Two Thousand Daffodils

To Mary, A lovely, charming lady + I'm proud to call "you" friend! Gayle

GAYLE SWEDMARK HUGHES

Wild Women Writers
An independent publishing company
Tallahassee, Florida

Two Thousand Daffodils

Cover photograph by Frank Hughes

ISBN: 978-0-9829015-4-0

Published by Wild Women Writers, Tallahassee, FL
www.wildwomenwriters.com

Wild Women Writers logo design by E'Layne Koenigsberg of 3 Hip
Chics, Tallahassee, FL, www.3HipChics.com

Printed in the United States of America

Dedication

To my husband who drove to St. Augustine to bring my reading glasses when I was in trial, who told me I was pretty when I was bald from chemotherapy and who brings out the best in me.

He is handsome, funny and smart—and has the kindest heart in the world.

Table of Contents

A little tale as hopeful as the daffodil itself . . .

Introduction

In some ways I have had a magical life. I have attended the College World Series as well as a national political convention. I learned to fly an airplane and became the mother of a wonderful man. I had an exciting career in the courtroom and dealt with famous people. I have been to Paris in the springtime and Portugal in the fall. I have studied at Oxford and seen the ancient cathedrals there. I was a law partner at age 27 with a former governor who had been a Supreme Court chief justice. I married the love of my life and explored the artistic and musical side of my nature later in life.

The place where I grew up, Amelia Island, is a barrier island off the coast of north Florida just south of Cumberland Island, Georgia. Indians camped here in 2000 B.C. Amelia Island has two towns: Fernandina, which boasted a population of 7,000 while I was in high school; and Amelia City, which had about 200 souls. The island has flown under eight flags since 1562 and has a rich colonial history that was instilled in us in childhood. It was named for Princess Amelia, third child of George II of England. In the 1500s there were Spanish missionaries and in the 1700s the English cultivated indigo here. The name Fernandina was the early name for Cuba and is still the name of one of the Galapagos Islands. Our town is named for King Ferdinand VII of Spain.

TWO THOUSAND DAFFODILS

At one time Fernandina was the busiest shipping port in the Western Hemisphere. The first cross-state railroad was from Fernandina to Cedar Key. Some of the early citizens were Sicilians with names like Salvador, Versaggi, and Poli. They started the modern shrimping industry here in Fernandina. Net making was established as a four-generation business by the Burbanks, whose daughter Charlene was my classmate and is my good friend. You will find a lot of old families of many different nationalities here. It is a cool town. My town. It was a place to have a Nancy Drew type existence with adventures at the fort on the north end of the island and explorations at the south end. We built huts from palmetto branches and pretended to be pirates. We carefully examined the bounty from the nets of the men who used to seine on the end of the island and we cooked our lunch over driftwood fires.

Not all was perfect and good. Some troubled parenting in my childhood left an imprint, and I had to marshal all of my strength and assets to be courageous in adult life. Daddy was smart, refined, elegant and gentle. Mother was brainy, histrionic, imaginative and beautiful. She was not nurturing. She did not want to have a child. She committed suicide.

I married a professor and my son, Lance Chandler Swedmark, loved beyond measure, was born. Later he and Frank, the love of my life, bonded while Lance was in the ninth grade and so, in many ways, Frank has parented with me. His son Jeff, an intelligent man who lives in Colorado Springs, is an integral part of our close family and I enjoy him immensely.

GAYLE SWEDMARK HUGHES

Frank is such a private person, and out of respect for him I have not included much about our meeting, courtship, and life together. To know me, however, is to realize that he has been a defining element of my happiness. He is, without question, the most unselfish person I have ever known. He is interested in everything in the universe and knows a good bit about a lot of it. Meeting him and marrying him has more than made up for any hurt or disappointment that ever came my way. When we became engaged, he planted two thousand daffodil bulbs in the meadow and along the driveway to celebrate our new beginning. I can see some of them from the window now. That is the title. Two Thousand Daffodils. The symbol of a fulfilled life. Hopefully a life well lived.

This then, is a sharing of some highlights of my life; a private and limited edition of my story. I hope that some family members and close friends will have a better understanding of my metamorphosis from the little child that I was. I hope they will be able to look at their own lives and appreciate that good, full, and healthy adults can develop from some troubled young ones.

At the beginning of the process, I wanted to write to understand who I am, who I once was, and what heritage I was born into. Later, as I wrote, I wanted to honor some of the ordinary people whose values I respect. I see them now as doing life-affirming work. God turns up occasionally as a governing presence. I have realized that we find manifestations of Grace in our history and also in our new friends. I honor those I remember as well as those I know

3

today.

It is a privilege to write for just one other person. I do it with gratitude and with pleasure. It is simply the story of how I evolved, day by day, year by year, from the scaredy-cat of childhood to the happy, mostly confident woman of seventy years of age. This is an invitation to join me on that journey.

A Hot Night in 1940

The north Florida heat was oppressive that September Friday as Laura Faye pulled her blue and white gingham maternity dress away from her legs and poured crowder peas into sterilized canning jars. Twenty-four pints of pole beans sat like little soldiers in the open window sills. Helping her mama put up vegetables in the tiny yellow farm kitchen was an annual ritual. A brown Philco radio on the counter was playing "Don't Fence Me In" by Bing Crosby and the Andrews Sisters.

Hitler was bullying his way across Europe as heavy bombs were being dropped over London, and the newsman interrupted sweet music to somberly announce that the Queen's apartments in Buckingham Palace had been hit.

"Mister" Sam Rayburn from Texas was newly elected Speaker of the House in Washington and with President Roosevelt was on a train to Jasper, Alabama, to attend the funeral of the late Speaker, William B. Bankhead.

Laura Faye wiped perspiration from her forehead with the back of her left hand and pinned the blond curls off her neck with her right hand. *Please, Lord, let this baby come soon!* she thought. She hoped to have a girl she could name after her own grandmother. Everett Council, her husband, was at work only four miles away over in Folkston, Georgia, on the north side of the St. Mary's River that divided Florida and Georgia. That's where the young couple lived. Everett served as Clerk of Court for Charlton County, Georgia, having been elected after the death of his father while he was serving in that position. Everett also had a budding little sawmill business he hoped to sell to a paper company someday.

A severe tropical storm hit at dusk on Saturday knocking out power just as the first labor contractions began for Laura Faye. The tiny white clapboard building called Sawyer Clinic was only a few miles from the courthouse where Saturday sessions were being held for a black man accused of stealing from the local car dealer. Advance notice was served to shut down the trial and also to let the hospital know that both a hurricane and a baby were due very soon. Everett and his brother-in-law Reginald helped to rig up a generator to provide power for the little hospital. There were six immaculate patient rooms and also a dirt parking lot full of relatives and friends awaiting an announcement from Laura Faye and Everett that their baby had arrived.

Back over on the Florida side of the river, Laura Faye's mother, Miss Cora, got out the dog-eared official family Bible (she had other copies of the King James edition in three rooms) and prepared to place the new entry on the fold-out tri-colored family tree. Her husband, Calvin Porter, got out the corn liquor in a brown paper bag, ready for the celebration of the birth of his first grandchild. He would invite his fishing pals, Mr. Henry Smith and Mr. Chris Walker, to join him outside by the truck when the time came. Drinking alcohol was not tolerated in Miss Cora's house.

Meanwhile, on the Georgia side of the river in a

6

Victorian home on Magnolia Street, Lilla, the maid; and Miss Naomi, the paternal grandmother-to-be; polished an antique silver baby spoon and added white eyelet and a satin pillow to the bassinette where the new baby would lay its tender little head.

At 5:35 p.m. on Sunday night Dr. Clayton Sawyer held the baby upside down and slapped. It was my own naked little bottom. I let out a healthy yell. Those folks there said it sounded just like "Hallelujah!"

Childhood Scenes

I have blurred memories of standing on the top of a horsehair sofa during the initial trip to Amelia Island to move in and have a vague impression of the slippery hardwood floors in the house. We had two houses together on the beach and a view of the Atlantic from the living room and the front porch. Daddy planted sun-tolerant flowers and we had a swing on our little front porch. Pre-school was mostly hunting for shells and playing with my dog. First grade was wonderful. I did work intensely on the first day without any break, thinking, *This is a little harder than I thought it would be.* As I took my workbook up to Mrs. Graham at the end of the day, she flipped through the pages in horror and yelled, "This was supposed to last you all year!" I had not quite finished it. Soon afterwards my parents and the principal, Mr. Kahler, had a talk and I was moved up to second grade.

One pleasant memory of childhood recurs in my dreams and has been verified as true. If I close my eyes, I can see it vividly now. The wind has the rain going sideways and it stings my face. I burrow down into the sand dune next to Bambi, my big collie. His fur is dry and soft and warm. I hide my face in him.

We are under a pier. It is getting dark. I have seen the coast guard search lights scanning the beach but do not know they are looking for me. Now I hear my name. Am I in trouble? It is best to be still and quiet. My parents think I am at Carolyn's house. It only started to get dark a little while ago. Bambi and I have taken a walk just like we always do, past our yard and the Seaside Inn and on down to the Gerbing's fishing pier. It is nice and cool and breezy. It is getting to be a little bit scary. Not too much. Bambi is not afraid of storms. This is a nice dry warm place up under the Gerbing's fishing pier in the sand dune tunnel. It feels safe. I like it a lot.

The voices and the flashlights are coming closer. There are three men in yellow slickers and goofy hats. The water is pouring on them now. A skinny man shouts, "I've got 'em." One man picks up Bambi and a smaller one lifts me up in his arms. I am six years old. They tell me they work for the coast guard and will take us in their big truck to see my parents. I tell them that Bambi is not allowed to ride in the car. The big man says, "Well, tonight he is." The man has wet hair and a nice big smile. They say we are in a hurricane.

The next strong impression was that of being in a war somewhere. I wasn't sure where or why. World War II was a vague reality in my world. German prisoners of war played baseball down the road from our house and did the famous "goose step" as they went out to the mound to bat and then played the rest of the game in normal fashion. One of my friends had real army helmets from an uncle. We used silk parachutes on the beach when we pretended to watch out for submarines in the area. Some enemy soldiers had been captured coming ashore about sixty miles away at Ponte Vedra Beach, so our play was made more real. Leon

9

LaChance got hold of an authentic army raft for us to play with, and I pretended to be captain and asked the boys, Leon and Jackie Reynolds, to paddle out to intercept enemy ships. In reality, these were shrimp boats off shore from our place. Our parents were livid and worried when we got out so far. We were confined to quarters, justifiably, for a few weeks.

Mother was "not well" during a lot of my childhood. On two occasions, the exact dates for which are lost to me, Daddy and I took Mama up to the University of Georgia Medical Center in Augusta to leave her for shock treatments. We drove up to Georgia in our grey Dodge and stayed in a dreary motel. Once we stayed in a tourist home where there were two beautiful Great Danes. I sat on the open porch and played with the dogs while my parents argued. It rained on the way home and I remember that there was no talking in the car. It was painful and lonely. Nobody ever asked me where mother was when I got home and nobody in the family ever talked about it. They may not have even known about it.

A Typical Day for a Nine Year Old

The day began by seeing Daddy off to work in a starched white shirt and tie with a breakfast prepared by me and eaten at our maple table, which now resides in my son and daughter-in-law's house. We rented out the beach house next door to ours and met everyone from opera singers to peanut farmers, mostly from Georgia. I was Cinderella, even at a young age, and had to clean the place each Sunday afternoon and put it in spotless order for the next summer tenant. After that, I was free to play. On a normal weekday our maid would clean our own house and I was off to meet my fellow pirates and play on the beach. We made sand castles with moats and turrets on the top with elaborate shell designs. We assigned duties and set about making a palmetto hut. We gathered driftwood for tables and used seaweed for floors. Our huts sometimes took a week, were admired by most, and vandalized overnight only rarely. When that happened, we simply started over.

With girlfriends the play was different. We made a stage in the double garage at our house, using the heavy wooden sliding doors as a curtain and fruit crates for a ticket booth. The charge was a dime for serious plays and fifteen cents for musicals. The boys we tried to draft for this game hated it, so we did the way Shakespeare had done and had one sex play all roles. We had a playhouse next door which I decorated with lantana in a jelly jar on a telephone cable spool table.

On shelves outdoors we displayed for sale pottery we made from our clay hills.

At our open house we served lemonade and thin sugar cookies made by Mrs. Gowen. It was all right that we had no video games to play and no television to watch. Our minds were fertile.

Grade School Crises

Freddy Derr from Chicago was a new student in our class and was extremely advanced socially. He kissed me when I was in the third grade. Carolyn said, "Where?"

"In the back of the auditorium," I said, "and it was really, really a bad kiss."

We immediately consulted our classmate Ruby Mixon, who knew literally everything worth knowing about boys and she said that it sounded like a French kiss. Most likely, she said, but not absolutely, I was pregnant.

We went into our bunker mentality. Carolyn said she would stand by me. She had saved $7 towards a blouse in a magazine ad and she was willing to give it to me and would help me find work. I couldn't tell my parents, but I did stop eating as much. They noticed and, thinking me ill, gave me Castoria. Then I was truly ill and this confirmed my pregnancy fears. I had heard that nausea was a symptom. Finally, I confided in my mother and, to her credit, she left the room to laugh. She explained that I was not pregnant. Life returned to some kind of normalcy.

Years later I ran into Fred and his wife at the Beach Club when they were visiting Fernandina for New Year's Eve. After a glass of champagne I told his wife the whole story. She thought it was hysterical and told him about it. Later in the evening he came up behind me and said, "Could I please try again?" I screamed and everybody at the table laughed.

This experience may have had an influence on my behavior during the high school and college years. Fear of pregnancy loomed big.

A terror of my youth was going over the rickety wooden bridge spanning the St. Mary's River between Georgia and Florida near my Mema's house. Going between the two worlds of my sets of grandparents required negotiating this water and I began to have horrible pains at the table at lunch when Mama or Daddy talked about going to see the other set of grandparents on the other side of the river. The palpitations were so bad that I imagined snakes in the top of my bedroom and poison in my milk. A common fear in those days was that the school bus window would fog up and I would miss my stop, that there would not be an empty seat in the classroom and I would be so embarrassed or that Susan Busby would find out I said her sister had cooties. Only the last was true. I overheard a conversation at the doctor's office while I was in the changing room. It gave me a certain cachet to know information about Sandra Busby and at recess I was proud to share it. Getting off the bus at 2:30 p.m. I was shocked to see my Daddy in work clothes, shirt and tie, Susan the older sister; and also Sandra's parents. The lecture to me that followed ended in tears for all and a sure threat from Susan. She promised me bodily harm if I ever said anything about her sister in the future. It had a profound effect on my dislike of gossip. To this day I tend to defend the object of any slur, real or imagined.

Fears mounted, along with the actual mental and occasional physical abuse at home. I told Daddy, who was so besotted by my mother, he refused to believe my tales. A kind sweet black woman named Anna intervened and took me aside. She said, more than once, "You are the Good Lord's happy child and you are loved. He is going to hold you in the palm of His hand." She gave me a clear glass prism to shine in the window to make a rainbow to remind me of God's love. Today it is a talisman on my bedroom night stand.

Musical Education Begins

Little did I know that the start of piano lessons would influence my entire life. The habit of work, the confidence in performing, the discipline to attain success, all had roots in this fortuitous encounter with "Aunt" Ruth.

Aunt Ruth is not really my aunt. She was my piano teacher and I have known and loved her since the time I was too young to reach the pedals of her shiny black Steinway. She had unruly curly hair the color of fire. Her little house was a board and batten behind the courthouse on Fifth Street. There was one concrete pot on each side of the steps. A few wilted caladiums or begonias would be in them most of the time, and in the fall, a few straggly mums. Twice a week I would walk from school on the irregular brick sidewalk lined with red bishop's caps, to her little house where I was greeted with lemonade and two store-bought cookies. Mother had made me promise not to ask for food or drink or to say I was hungry, but I always was. There was a plaque over her living room archway that said "Music is love, in search of a word." The *House Beautiful* designers would have considered it gauche or tacky, but to me it was magnificent. The entrance to West Point could not have inspired me more.

Aunt Ruth said her husband Fred was a devout alcoholic. He would sometimes fall out of bed with a crashing sound. Undaunted, she would simply say, "That's just Fred." They were a strange and unlikely couple and we would never have had her European-trained talent in our little town had she not met and fallen for Fred, who worked for the paper mill, timber division. I was glad that he had brought her to us.

After seven years of lessons, Aunt Ruth said she had taken me as far as she could and sent me to a German lady, Dr. Marcellus, to study music theory and harmony. I hated the monkeys in the Marcellus house and the mean manner and probably the lack of love and cookies, and so after a year I was back to Aunt Ruth. She taught me then how to draw notes on staff paper and to do rudimentary composing to prepare me for being a composition major at FSU. I now had another security blanket to add to my arsenal of confidence. The clear glass prism from Anna was reinforced by Aunt Ruth's abiding friendship and gift of music.

Every time I returned to Fernandina I saw her. Sometimes I stayed with her because Fred had died and she was a little lonely. We played duets and she sang operettas to me in her strong powerful voice. Later, when I went back there on business, I took her out to supper. She came to my trials and once the judge had to caution her not to clap when I finished my opening statement. The last time I saw her she took me to see the organ at St. Michaels Catholic Church where she had a job as organist. She was Presbyterian but the Catholics paid better. One of my favorite memories with her is slipping into that gorgeous place and listening to her play Bach and Schubert, which echoed across the courtyard of statues and graves. Then, with a wicked smile, she launched into "Proud Mary" and other popular tunes. Surely the neighborhood was wide awake when we left. Aunt Ruth died in her sleep a month later. She must have been a welcome sight to the heavenly choir.

Roots

Aunt Ruth knew Daddy's family and talked to me about a great-great aunt who was brave and had taught black folks to read when the men in the family mocked her and opposed her. It gave me some idea that courage had been sent to me in my veins and was passed down somehow.

I learned family history like most Southern children, at reunions, weddings, and funerals. Photographs wrapped in tissue and ribbon were brought out. Legends were passed down. It wasn't a question of money. It was a part of a person's place in history. My cousin John Bentley Mayes, art critic for *The Toronto Globe and Mail*, has written a most accurate and unsentimental account of the family that is incomparable. *Power in the Blood* (HarperCollins Publishers, 1997) took years of research and a talent for separating the myth of the South from the reality. Quite a bit of my information came from that source.

On a pilgrimage to the Carolinas and Virginia ten years ago, I covered the geography of over two hundred years of my family history. Rarely did I see the popular modern imagination's Old South. Only in Mayesville, South Carolina, when I visited the home of its founder Matthew Peterson Mayes, my great-great, grandfather.

The usual date given by historians for emergence of the Old South is 1830. It was over by 1861. The historian Louis Wright said that time wasted brilliant minds fighting for the futile and brought forth one of the worst deadly sins: pride. Even more terrible, it led the whole South to ruin.

Matthew Peterson Mayes was born wealthy in 1794 near Emporia, south of Petersburg, Virginia. His mother was second cousin to Thomas Jefferson and it is clear they visited each other's homes. His family had prospered on the banks of the Appomattox River for more than a hundred years before the Revolution. There Matthew sat watching schooners loaded with tobacco heading for overseas. A restless nineteen year old, he went off to fight in America's second war of independence from Britain in 1814. Seeking excitement and adventure, he apparently also found romance and took a new bride to the site of what is today Mayesville. He laid out a plan for the town on Carolina dirt.

In the early 1980s two cousins of mine, Joel Chandler and Rutledge Dingle, along with John Bentley, discovered a copy of the original map for Mayesville by traveling south from Raleigh on Interstate 95 which follows roughly the same route Matthew Peterson Mayes took on his first trip there. The map showed the outer limit of the town by a circle. At the top of the circle is the home place of Matthew. From this point there extends radial avenues across the circle. One leads to the house of Dr. Junius Alceus Mayes, the squire's first son. All of the children were named after famous Roman orators and Greek satirists. Another avenue went to the house of Thomas Alexander Mayes, my own great-grandfather, his second son. When the trains first started coming to Mayesville, they could recognize the town by the early morning fire burning at the Thomas Alexander house.

I was able, one April morning in the 1990s, to drive up the dirt lane to that house and meet the new owner, a Virginia architect. I gave him some of the original hardware for his restoration of the place, including the manual bell ringer for the middle front door. He invited me to sit in my grandmother's childhood bedroom and look out the broad windows to the orchard beyond. I walked in her steps on the wooden floors to the side porch where she danced as a teenager, and down the steps where she had thrown her bridal bouquet and said goodbye to her family. She moved to Folkston, Georgia, with her husband and never returned except once to carry her little son Warren Baird on the train to the Mayesville family cemetery.

Through the research of cousin John Bentley Mayes, I discovered the Old Salem Black River Church, a pre-revolutionary gem with incomparable history and beauty of classic architecture. When my cousin Regina Dukes and I visited there, it had recently been hit by hurricane Hugo and the roof was damaged. An anonymous donation of the precise repair bill had been made the preceding week. When I was introduced to the congregation as the great-great granddaughter of Matthew Peterson Mayes, the reception was uncommonly warm. The greeting was effusive and as I graciously received the welcome my cousin whispered to me, "You know that they think you are the anonymous benefactor, don't you?" Regina, from a different side of my family, was a good sport about reading maps and helping me maneuver around South Carolina, but that day I simply could not have done without her support.

I asked for directions to the ladies room. A well-dressed woman of a certain age said to me, "Oh, my dear! That would spoil the architectural integrity of this structure." Regina grabbed my hand and pulled me out back to the cemetery saying, "There is no cemetery in the South that doesn't have a privy in the back of it!" Sure enough, through cobwebs, birds' nests, and the tombstones of Henrietta and her descendants, we found our destination. Mice scurried out as we arrived.

The Chandler families and the Council line in my family history have important and useful lives, but the Mayes family has such a well-documented story that I selected it for this particular effort. Also, there are such interesting characters in that family lineup. Cousin Elma is an example of the courage, grit and gentility that identified that clan.

Cousin Elma

Cousin Elma's house is the big old empty Victorian on Saint Charles Street in Mayesville with the peeling paint and the overgrown yard. Grapevines and kudzu climb up the windows since she died. She never would have tolerated that. She kept a neat home and was sweet and gracious to every person she saw. She was my grandma Gammy's first cousin and, therefore, my third. In South Carolina that counts for a lot. Cousin Elma, a delicate beauty with fine curly black hair and violet eyes, suffered quietly through serious illnesses. She sat by the side of the sick and gave to those who needed her. She always had a fresh lace handkerchief for the heartbroken to cry on at funerals. Her own husband, Dr. Clinton Wakefield Davidson, died while I was living on the west coast so I didn't attend the funeral. Gammy sent me the notice.

A yellowed newspaper clipping slipped out of my Bible yesterday and I remembered something. The headline read "Prominent physician struck down in his home by bandits." I know better.

On the front porch at Gammy's house back in 1961, surrounded by ferns and ornamental pepper plants, two ladies rocked and fanned themselves with paper fans from Hardee's Funeral Home and talked. I was on the settee in the middle sitting room napping and reading. I could hear them easily through the screen door.

"You know," said Gammy, "our dear Elma never knew that Dr. Davidson was stepping out on her with another woman." She continued, "When she came downstairs late that night in her robe and slippers to answer the bell, a tall bearded dark man just asked for Dr. Davidson. Cousin Elma thought it was another sick person who needed help. She offered tea so her husband could have time to get dressed. The man said, 'No, thank you.' She went upstairs to get her husband and he came down directly.

"A gunshot echoed through the stairwell and when she jumped up to run see what happened she saw her husband, Dr. Davidson, lying in the open doorway and the man was gone. He was arrested three days later.

"Cousin Elma attended the trial in her navy linen dress and short white gloves and her navy pumps. The defense was that Dr. Davidson was the paramour of the accused's wife Sophie. I declare, I do not know what the truth is even today. The woman, Sophie, testified that she had made up the story to make her own husband jealous. The sheriff, Elma's first cousin, said that he had not checked the weapon for fingerprints. The first time that had ever happened in his twenty-nine years as a law officer.

"Cousin Elma was dignified and warmly greeted all who came to the home after the trial," Gammy finished her tale. "She served tea, watercress sandwiches and the Lady Baltimore cake her friends had baked."

After the acquittal, the defendant came to work at Cousin Elma's mercantile store.

Daddy

Everett Council Smith, my Daddy, was kind and gentlemanly. My girlfriends told me later that he was their "ideal man" and the guys told me they thought he was the epitome of manners. My English teacher said she thought he looked like Stewart Granger and sounded like Gregory Peck. She had a crush on him. Daddy was always true blue to mother. He was totally besotted and hypnotized by her. That was his only fault that I knew of. If it is a fault. Because he could never see how she really was, it is difficult to write about him, even today.

He was from a fine old family living in genteel poverty when I was in grammar school, but in his preteen years he wore the clothes and lived in the house that some people wanted. When the Depression hit in his teen years and his beloved father died of a brain tumor, he went to work supporting the three widowed aunts and his mother who now depended upon him. The savings were all gone. Wiped out. His entire family's annual income, once near $100,000 per year, dwindled to the few dollars that could be made from a garden plot, the pecan groves on the grounds and the boarders who could be housed in the extra bedrooms in Gammy's home.

I wasn't there, of course, but the friends who knew him said that he never complained. He arose at 4 a.m. and drove the truck to Racepond, near Waycross, Georgia. He and three of the hired hands (who previously worked on the place and now were unemployed just like daddy) started a sawmill on a small piece of property that the family had salvaged. Though the helpers were black gentlemen, they were as caring as family and took turns with Daddy catching a nap on the way up to Racepond. Sometimes the youngest one would have a head in Daddy's lap as he drove. Eventually a larger sawmill business, owned by the Johnson brothers in Folkston, Georgia, bought him out and he became the bookkeeper part time while he served as Clerk of Court for Charlton County, Georgia.

Later, a paper company bought out the new larger sawmill and Daddy became office manager and then manager. He went to Washington State and worked for Rayonier Canada, a subsidiary of ITT. At the time of his retirement, he was assistant comptroller living in New York City.

As a daddy he was infinitely patient, gluing back broken dolls and ceramics, custom building furniture for my bedroom and painting my bookcases with seven coats of finish. When I had a wreck in the old 1949 Ford during some tense labor negotiations at the mill, he simply got up from his bargaining table when I waved to him, and came to me quietly to say, simply, "Princess, are you all right? Then we have nothing to worry about." He was also a stalwart Atticus Finch type when his company had an essay contest, with only coded numbers on the papers in lieu of names to eliminate favoritism. When a black man won, someone said, "Well, we cannot give this to that young man, that is for sure!" Daddy said, "Well, then, you can find yourself a new president." He personally presented the award at the Rotary Club to huge applause.

When I said "I may want to be a nurse," he said, "Why not be a doctor?" When I said I thought it would be fun to be a flight attendant, his response was "How 'bout a pilot?" Yes, dads are a huge influence. Thank you, Daddy.

Our Mothers

Entering high school, I had added one more building block in the mental health substructure. Adding to my clear glass prism reflecting sunbeams in the window, I had the basic training, discipline and confidence gained from years of music lessons in Aunt Ruth's little bungalow.

I also had the encouragement from my father that I could do absolutely anything I wanted to do if I worked hard and planned for it. Mother also let me know that women could do more than the current climate allowed and that I should use my brain in case any opportunity ever came up. To the best of my memory, none of our mothers worked outside the home.

It was the time of Eisenhower, aprons, fried pork chops, and the Lone Ranger. Our moms approximated June Cleaver to some extent although we later discovered that skeletons lurked behind the wallpapered kitchen facade. Meanwhile our moms attended cooking schools at the theater sponsored by Tip Top Bread. They came home with door prizes of flour scoops or white plastic measuring spoons. They played their parts well.

Incredibly, in light of what we know today, most of our Moms smoked, usually unfiltered Chesterfields. Even some of the Baptists smoked. As our mothers marched off to the beach each summer morning to tan themselves while we made sand castles, they emphasized style in dress.

The sunglasses, coolers full of martinis, the hat and the one piece Rose Marie Reid swimsuit and shoes all matched. Usually they were in shades of kelly green or electric blue. In a bow to individuality my best friend Carolyn's mom took her peas to shell at the beach. She prepared forty percent of her evening meal while basking in the sun.

Mrs. Oxley, Carolyn's mother, was very serious in her devotion to cooking for us. When I spent the night at Carolyn's house, no matter what time we awoke, whether it be nine or eleven on Saturday morning, she was at the ready to prepare our breakfast. The spatula was high in her hand as soon as our toes hit the floor. She was such a caretaker that even at our twentieth class reunion I noticed that she had taped a note on Carolyn's Crown Royal bottle for the BYO party. It said, "This is the property of Carolyn Oxley."

My own mother was not born to serve children. We always had a maid, as did most people I knew. The movie *The Divine Secrets of the Ya Ya Sisterhood* best portrays her, except that she had few women friends. The mood would strike her, once in a while, to cook. When she did, it was magnificent. She was the first person I ever knew in our circle of friends to use fresh herbs. She cut them up in scrambled eggs and added them to soups. She scooped out oranges and filled them with sweet potatoes. She scalloped the edges to make them pretty. The one time I remember her waiting on me when I was ill, she made tiny strips of cinnamon toast and served them with chamomile tea. As she walked out of my yellow bedroom with the crossed dotted-Swiss curtains, she said, "Peter Rabbit's mama used to give him that." I was thrilled. A memory to treasure.

When she wasn't cooking, I made meals for Daddy from chicken or pork with a generous portion of candied apple slices featured in *American Girl* magazine. At age nine I was a fairly accomplished cook for simple meals.

Two Praying Grandmothers

Whatever is good about me and whatever fortune has come to me must be a result of my two remarkable grandmothers and their total devotion to me. They were complete opposites except that both had an abiding faith and both prayed for me every single day.

Naomi, the eldest grandmother, was my Daddy's mom. She was born Naomi Ionia Mayes in Mayesville, S.C. They had a home, too, in Charleston, S.C., where she and others of her time said that the Ashley and the Cooper Rivers joined to form the Atlantic Ocean. She was baptized in a church that was established before the American Revolution. She studied poetry and elocution as a young lady. Her mother and grandmother, against violent opposition from the men in the family, started a school for black young ladies and taught Mary McCleod Bethune. Mary McCleod later founded a college in Florida called Bethune-Cookman.

Naomi, or Gammy as I called her, was genteel. She wore pale lavender and alice blue and usually a cameo brooch on a velvet ribbon at her neck. She was so tenderhearted that she asked if she could take her husband's former fiancé on their honeymoon because she felt sorry for her. She also lost all seven of her children except Daddy to scarlet fever and smallpox, yet she remained loving and kind and never lost her faith.

She polished her little silver iced tea spoons with a cloth

in her lap. She stirred up pound cakes by hand. She read poetry and watered her ferns and pepper plants. She rocked on the porch. She sometimes washed scuppernong grapes and put them in a spatter ware bowl for us to eat on the porch while we listened to the trains go by at night and told stories. She prayed for me every day. I was her only grandchild.

Cora, my maternal grandmother, was a cat of a different color. Called Mema by me, she was born Cora Civility Higginbotham and was of hardy peasant stock. She lost her mother before age five and learned to cook for field hands, reading books when she could sneak them into the hayloft. She could clean a fish, sew up a coat, and wring a chicken's neck to start supper. She was fearless. She was dauntless. One of my favorite memories is of visiting my mother in New York City with her. As a treat we went to the United Nations dining room.

Before we left the apartment, Laura Faye, my mother, said to Mema, "You need to get dressed. Maybe you want to wear your new blue suit. Gayle and I are taking you to the United Nations building to eat. You will love it, Mama. It is right next to the East River in the Turtle Bay neighborhood."

"Well, well," Mema said. "Don't know if I like to eat all that foreign food. Anyhow, it will be something to tell my Sunday school class about, won't it?"

As we walked up the plaza steps past the statues and the flags from different countries, I said, "Gosh, Mema, I feel special being out with you and my mother. Isn't this a beautiful day?"

Then seated at the lovely table we tried our lobster salad and chilled soup. Mema said, "This is the best mayonnaise I have ever tasted! I think we need to get their recipe."

"Please," Laura Faye said. "They simply do not give out recipes at the United Nations dining room."

Mema, looking slightly chagrined, changed the subject. I told her we would take a harbor tour later in the day and maybe shop at Lord and Taylor for an Easter dress for her. My mother and I left the table to refresh our makeup in the ladies room and take a look at the decor there.

Eventually, as we returned to the table, we were surprised to see a tall man in a starched entree chef's jacket with a mandarin collar and a white torque-style hat standing next to Mema. She said, proudly, "Chef Anton, I want you to meet my daughter and granddaughter. And, oh yes, thank you so much for that wonderful mayonnaise recipe."

She was never uncomfortable in any situation, no matter how unusual for her.

Mema belonged to a little country church called Buford Grove, which was the center of her social life. She read her Bible first thing in the morning and right after lunch before her rest. When I took the obligatory afternoon nap in her little bedroom with the chenille bedspread, the windows would be open and an oscillating fan pulled fresh air across the window sill. I could hear the radio soap operas in the background and the whirl of her treadle sewing machine. I would awake with a ridge on my face from the chenille imprint on summer skin. On my sixteenth birthday she gave me a white leather Bible with my name in gold. She prayed for me every day of her life.

In a newspaper article about her, Mema is described by Claudine Braddock for the *Charlton County Herald* as having a countenance "as serene as the gentle St. Mary's River that flows near her home in Boulogne."

Mema described the train ride they had to take the four miles from Florida across the St. Mary's to Folkston, Georgia, where she did her shopping. It cost a dime. She said, "Times were so much sweeter back then." In the old days, she said, we helped all our neighbors. We sat with the sick who needed it.

She said that her darkest hour was when the Navy plane of her son, Calvin Jr., crashed 57 miles out from Mayport, Florida, into the ocean. He was not quite twenty years old. The fighting had ended in Europe and Japan would soon surrender. There is a WWII statue at the shrimp docks in Fernandina at the end of main street with Uncle Calvin's name under the Navy section. It is nice to take the young members of the family to see it.

Mema had a painless heart attack while getting dressed for Sunday night service at church. She was life-flighted to Baptist Memorial in Jacksonville where she told the staff that she was so surprised they could not offer her cold apple juice at such a nice facility. She ate chicken and rice and closed her eyes and died just short of her one hundredth birthday. She was buried at her beloved Buford Grove cemetery.

Two grandmas, so different. So powerful and loving. Lucky me. I know that they both gave me an insulation against harm. When I try to explain to people why I am not damaged much from the childhood trauma that I suffered, I have to include Mema and Gammy in that explanation.

Mema's Cozy Kitchen

In the home of my maternal grandmother, the kitchen was full of warmth and encouragement to a would-be chef. There was a red plastic rooster clock on the wall and an oilcloth table cover on the little formica dinette set in Mema's kitchen. A bottle of pepper sauce and a decanter of cane syrup were always on the table. The faded wallpaper had dishes and spoons and forks on a plaid background. Mason jars full of bread and butter pickles lined her white metal pie safe. The cotton café curtains had a border of cherries on green stems.

The room, on the northwest rear of her little white frame house, sat next to a large screened sleeping porch. From the sink you could see the smokehouse where sausages and pork hams were hung. You could see the hen house and a wild orange tree with its gnarly inedible green oranges next to the cane mill.

Cane was a staple with rural Southern families. We children stood silently outside Mema's kitchen in the barnyard to watch the grinding process of pressing the juice out of cane. Older kids were allowed to feed the stalks into the mill where the juice would then pour into a barrel. A "sweep" or long pole was attached to the mill and to a dusty old mule that turned the mechanism as he walked around in a slow circle looking bored.

Strong men lifted the barrels up and took them to the

huge black cast iron pot under Mema's shed where the juices were boiled down. The aroma of the wood-fire under the pot cooking down 40-plus gallons of pure cane juice was pleasant. The froth off the boiling cane juice was fed to the hogs and made them knee-walking drunk. A smaller version of the black pot, once used for starching clothes, sits in my yard today and holds firewood.

Mema had spatter ware bowls for making cobbler from the berries we picked on her fences, a big porcelain dishpan for making cathead buttermilk biscuits, light as clouds, and the ubiquitous cast iron skillet, which was heated hot as can be before pouring cornbread mixture into it. In my younger days she let me churn butter. Never have I tasted better. Later, she had me put the orange color packet into purchased margarine. A powerful dairy lobby wouldn't dare let it be sold already colored and looking like butter. No worries. It never tasted as divine as the real thing.

The aroma of vanilla extract or citrus being peeled greeted you no matter what time of day you surprised her in that kitchen. At various times I brought friends, a new baby or a neighbor. There was always a "little bite" to eat.

Ms. Julia Child has a kitchen in the Smithsonian. Mema's is, in its own way, memorialized by being forever embedded in the memory of anyone of us who ever walked through those heart pine doors. It was a place for confiding secrets as we washed dishes together by hand. It was a place for feeling totally welcome and at peace. It was a critical part of my early security.

Church Camp at Camp O'Leno

Our church sent the eighth graders through senior highs each summer to a camp near Lake City, Florida. It was built of sturdy timbers by WPA construction workers from the Depression and had a beautiful mess hall on the Santa Fe River with open porches and timbered rafters as well as individual cabins scattered through the woods. It also had a swinging bridge across the river. The church camp gave me an understanding that there was a whole group of people who were fun and popular and who were Christians. It deepened my faith to know these people. It had a strong effect on me when I was initiated during an impressive ceremony into the order of the Bronze Maid.

I recall the night when we were tapped on the shoulder in our sleep and taken down to the river. Each person to be initiated was in a canoe, in a white dress, with a crown of fresh vines and flowers. There was only the sound of the Sante Fe River rapids downstream and a few night birds calling out. Moonlight shone through the pine trees of the park. I could barely make out the big sturdy timbers of the mess hall on the hill.

A deep mellow voice emerged from the top of the suspension bridge: "You have been chosen as a symbol of the best of womanhood. You have shown qualities of leadership, virtue, and respect for your fellow campers. You are invited tonight into the sacred Circle of the Bronze Maids of the

Osceola Forest. Just as Indian maidens of years ago lived in these woods, may you always return and recall the lessons learned. As you pass under the bridge, and become a bronze maid, may the spirit of these woods remain with you."

There was singing across the way. Flower blossoms were tossed on us as we slowly coasted under the bridge holding our tall candles in a glass vase of water and honeysuckle vines. A night to remember. I guess the spirit of those woods did remain.

The memories are vivid. If I close my eyes at night when I want to go to sleep, I can smell and feel the place.

The rain was hitting the tin roof on my little log cabin at a pretty good clip. Yvonne Devane, from Lake City, our counselor said, "No talking. It is ten o'clock, girls." Our church camp was pretty strict. The night before I had gotten in trouble for going out on the swinging bridge with some other children so we could shine flashlights on the counselors sitting on the river bank below, on the off chance we could catch them actually kissing a date. The counselors and craft teachers and staff went out sometimes when we little kids were in bed. My archery instructor Melvin Pope had a crush on the piano player for vespers. They sometimes sat together. Once he lifted me up over the river and said, "Little girl, do you want to see how your flashlight works under the water?" But he didn't hurt me. Everyone laughed.

My heroine of all of the camp was June Conyers, who embodied the ideal womanhood qualities of beauty and virtue. This was 1952 and 1954 before the explicit lyrics of today's music and the libertine life style of some of our sisters and brothers. Lucky for me, she was my counselor the first time I ever went to camp and then, again, four years later. June, pretty blonde daughter of noted Presbyterian minister Dr. Conyers, had a sweet smile. She was a talented pianist. She took time out of whatever she was doing to listen to questions or problems of campers. I saw her interrupt her music practice to help a camper tie a certain knot for his sailing class. She was patient and accepting of the faults and mistakes of others. She was modest and gave credit to others. I wish I had more of her qualities. She married the son of camp director, Dr. Ed Montgomery, Sr., and he also became a Presbyterian minister, the Rev. Ed Montgomery, Jr.

I saw her at a Camp O'Leno reunion several years ago and was happy to tell the campers gathered there what she had meant to me.

After I finally got to sleep, I had to get up once to make a trip to the restrooms in a separate building, also log, and quite a walk. It was across the pine straw and tree roots with the scary night sounds of owls and bobcats in those woods near High Springs, Florida. The open pavilion was also constructed of huge logs. Next day was the talent show. My job was to play the music for the group singing and also to introduce the acts. I was also in two of the skits.

My friend Isabel Mott, an absolutely gorgeous girl of fourteen, was to do an interpretive dance. We found her some black tights and a black turtleneck shirt. It was all in good taste except that whatever she wore would stop traffic.

I had another good friend, Hugh Augustus Wilson, from Lake City who attended Bolles Academy in Jacksonville during the school year and sometimes came over to Fernandina to visit me. He also played the trumpet very, very well and so I asked him if he would play for Isabel's dance. He finally agreed to perform W.C. Handy's classic "St. Louis Blues." Isabel swayed to the horn music and kicked to the rafters in a slow graceful movement. She danced on a dark stage with backlighting emphasizing the rhythm of her interpretation. Hugh's notes were perfect. "I hate to see, that evening sun go down, 'cause my lovin' baby done left this town." Oh, yeah!

Obviously, this was the winning act. They completely broke up the camp and took a few bows. Dr. Montgomery, our preacher, cleared his throat a couple of times but agreed that it was nicely done. I heard that Isabel and Hugh saw each other in later years. I saw Hugh often in college at FSU. I haven't kept up with them since.

Poliomyelitis

Rumors spread like wildfire about a new disease. The days, weeks, and months of the polio epidemic are vivid to me because our neighborhood felt it so intimately.

One afternoon the phone rang with news that Bobby Mertz, three doors down, had come home with a stiff neck and a high fever. Bobby was tall and good-looking, with dark brown hair and eyelashes any woman would envy. He had the strong tan arms of the good baseball player that he was. His humor was a little sarcastic, but dry, and right on the money.

We weren't best friends, but did find time to slide down the sand dunes near our houses together and played volleyball in his yard with other friends. One day he had a stiff neck and then by night he was paralyzed.

The next call on our big black telephone brought the news that Mrs. Borlew down the road had some bad disease. That evening the television news, then only fifteen minutes, was devoted entirely to the "polio scare." We were told that the disease had been around in some form for years but that this was a severe and dangerous strain. Public water fountains were to be avoided. Our sports events and movie theatres were closed or cancelled until further notice The circus was cancelled. Handouts at church warned us not to sit close together, not to get overheated and to avoid sharing food and drink. We were told that the warm months were usually the worse.

Newsreels at the movie theatres showed children in iron lungs and wheelchairs and on crutches from the disease. President Roosevelt was a fund raiser for the disease in his later years, and was thought to have contracted it at Campobello Island in Canada in 1921 although research now indicates he may have had Guillain-Barre Syndrome rather than polio.

Sister Kenny, an Australian bush nurse, invented new forms of physical therapy for victims. Doctors Salk and Sabin did a great service to humanity when they developed various forms of vaccine for the dreaded disease that had us in its grips in the early 1950s.

I stayed in my room a lot during the polio epidemic. Normally I had stayed in my room alone for a good part of my life, anyway, listening to the radio and reading or playing records on my small record player. I read a lot. Nancy Drew and the little Golden Guide nature books were my favorites. My bedroom was pleasant. There were pennants on the wall from favorite schools, a pine bookcase made by Daddy, and the glass prism in a sunny spot. Yellow dotted Swiss curtains framed the windows. Baseball memorabilia was all over the place. On the east wall there was my piano. I had nice thick white shag rugs on my hardwood floors. It felt a pleasant place to be. Usually, it was a safe place to be.

Summer at the Dixieland Dimestore

In the summer of 1956 we all worked. I was allowed one day to sleep forever when school let out for the vacation and then the next day I had better be up and about looking for a job. Family always agreed to match whatever small wages I earned. My parents were both very concerned about my not being lazy or spoiled. Since all of my friends had to work during vacation, it was more fun than not, a kind of mark of maturity. We all volunteered during the winter at nearby Hope Haven Polio Hospital. I worked during the school year after cheerleader practice at the Recreation Center passing out locker keys.

A phone call came from Carolyn Oxley early the second day of vacation: "Dixieland Dimestore is hiring five girls today." Carolyn set up an appointment for me, Rachel, Betty Ann Cosson and Phyllis Harold. By noon we were there in the store in our hose and heels with our hair tucked under in pageboys or up in neatly pinned ponytails.

Orvis, the manager, who had a terrible ill-fitting toupee and tobacco breath, kept Camels in his shirt pocket. You could see through the fabric on his nylon shirt and actually read the letters. As he told us we were hired, I was glad to be in the back of the group. He said, "Ladies, you will not sit during working hours. You will begin at 9 a.m., take a half hour for lunch, no supper break except fifteen minutes to eat what you brought to work, and you will leave promptly at 9 p.m. after making sure your area is clean and neat. You will receive seventy-five cents per hour and we will have to deduct for any items you break or allow customers to break."

Orvis was constantly trying to get girls to go back in the storage room to "help look for items," but we all avoided him like the plague. Phyllis had to slap him and got him to behave by threatening to tell his wife, who ran the hat shop next door and had tight little red curls. The store owner never knew of our plight since sexual harassment complaints had not yet been popularized and we needed the work.

I was assigned to selling 45 rpm records and played "Jim Dandy to the Rescue" over the loud speaker out on the street until people actually complained about it. Then I switched to constantly playing "Tutti Fruiti" by Pat Boone.

Carolyn had the perfume counter, surrounded by displays of Evening in Paris perfume with its little blue bottle and silk tassel. She also sold a new product called "Atomic Bomb" perfume which was trendy and a big seller. Betty Ann was in toys and let anyone play with anything. We had to pitch in sometimes to pay for things the poorest little kids would break. I think Rachel sold goldfish.

If we were tired and tried to lean against the counter to take the weight off, Orvis would jump up and "clap clap" with his hands and frown.

After work the first week Mama told me that a wonderful handsome boy was on the phone and wanted to go to a special party. I told her to tell him I was going to go soak in the tub and then sleep. This experience, I am positive, helped me to value an education.

Anis and Her Fortune Telling

My trust in fortune telling took a major hit when I saw that Sister Fay's business sign was underwater. Why she didn't know that her yard was going to flood out? My dad said that the only thing she could tell for sure is that she would be a dollar richer when you left.

In the 1950s in Fernandina we had old Anis who was much better at predicting the future. Nostradamus she was not, but she was pretty good at foretelling the scores in the local football games. Anis gave our players a confidence that was part of a self-fulfilling prophecy of success. More than one Pirate victory can be credited to her predictions to the guys.

Her old rickety house was down on 6th and Elm Street toward the paper mill. She had a dozen cats. When a limb of her Japanese plum tree or loquat tree hit the edge of her roof or fruit landed there during a session, it scared the fillings out of your teeth. To add to the drama, we were to come as close to midnight as possible and had to go upstairs one at a time for our reading. Anis would be lying in bed under an old faded quilt. She had a machete across her lap for protection and long black braids in her hair.

She told me that I would marry twice to blond men from up North. She said I would be happy the second time. To burst the bubble, Daddy pointed out that after all I did live in Florida and so most people would live north of me.

He said that Anis wouldn't still be alive when I came for a refund. In fact, I did marry two blond men from north of my town. My husband Frank, though, the love of my life, is only from as far north as Alabama.

My best friend Carolyn tried to fool Anis by putting on George Boland's class ring. Anis wasn't fooled. She said, "That ring does not belong to you or your boyfriend, but the boy it belongs to is out in the car." Odds? Who knows? She may have had a microphone outside. She was a smart old character.

The ceremony of going there was most of the fun. Being so scared on Halloween night was more than worth the fifty cents fee to have Anis predict the future. Mostly she spoke of pleasant futures, omitting the illnesses, heartbreak and lost loves that would face all of the class. Maybe it is a fortunate thing that she wasn't able to truly tell all of us our futures. We may have been afraid to face them.

Something To Leave Out or To Keep In

It is disgusting to me to see people go on the television or other media and tell every detail of their personal lives. The claim is that it is good for others to share that information. I have been extremely careful in this memoir to avoid hurting others and bringing up difficult times in their lives or in describing the alleged weaknesses of others to make my own life seem more noble. There is, however, one incident that I need to include because I have an obligation to be honest about my life and it also points out how so-called respectable people can slide off the rails and do despicable things. I have since found, to my amazement, that almost everyone has at least one incident like this. Perhaps it will encourage others to know that it is not necessarily life defining. Describing it in a way that is designed to keep it from being creepy to the reader and yet not sanitizing it too much is a difficult task.

When I was between my twelve and thirteenth birthdays, I was babysitting for children. Sometimes I took them to the beach. One day my mother told me that a lady wanted me to stay with her during the night when her husband would be away. My mother thought I should do it and there would be a good hourly rate. I would go to school as normal the next day and it would only be for one night. I agreed.

After I got settled there that evening about dark, I was told by the husband that she was resting and not to disturb her. A professional and respected businessman, he was leaving for a meeting in Jacksonville. I read my homework, went to sleep. During the night I was awakened abruptly by the husband. It was completely dark but I recognized his voice and did not like the way it sounded or that he was wrestling with me. Some force that I do not know to this day helped me to finally fight him off. Screaming, I ran to the wife's room for help. She was not there. Her bed was made.

I locked myself in her room and called my own house. Daddy answered and I told him to come get me, that I was ill and had a stomach problem. I ran out of the house and was standing in the driveway when he arrived.

He said, "Are you all right?"

I said, "Yes, I just need to lose my cookies."

He stopped and I did. He asked if I wanted to go to the doctor.

"No," I said. "I just want to go home and get in my own bed." When I got home, mother asked me what was wrong and I told her the same thing. While this incident was legally an attempted sexual battery, and, thank God, not a completed sexual battery, it is clear that charges should have been filed. I have no idea how many others this happened to. He remained a pillar in our community and every time I rode by his house I wanted to burn it down. I recently heard an actual rape victim make this statement and I totally understood what he meant. The event was bad enough that it makes me have goose bumps to type this. It was bad enough that I had nightmares, the cliché nightmares for victims, for years. Once in a while they return. Thankfully, though, it wasn't nearly as bad as it could have been. When I was in high school, he came up to me on the sidewalk downtown next to Allan's Department Store and gave me a wrapped gift. I tossed it in the trash bin next to us at the corner. He put his head down and walked away. He is dead now.

On balance, this kind of thing is better confronted than avoided. It is best not to be a passive player in someone else's life but rather a young woman taking charge of her own life. It is best to let young women know that they are not alone. That most people have this kind of experience. We are not victims. We have survived those fallible people who tried to control us. We have endured and even thrived to get on with our lives.

Sarah Alice's Island

As you ride across the bridge to Amelia Island, Florida, you will glimpse pines floating in sawgrass down below you on the right side. Natives have always called it Sarah Alice's Island. She was a local legend.

A mysterious creature, Sarah Alice was not beautiful but rather leathery, scrawny and wiry. We didn't know much about her except that supposedly she had foreign checks deposited to her account at the old Florida National Bank on Centre Street and she was rumored to be related to British royalty.

She sure didn't seem to need much of that money. A few times a year you could spot her slowly making her way across the old drawbridge going to town for supplies. She was barefoot, dressed in a croker sack kind of outfit and carrying a cloth bag over her shoulder.

Sarah Alice spoke to a very few. She always talked to the bridge tender. Once she spoke to me for a few minutes. Who knows why? She talked to David Stone and to my piano teacher. It was a badge of distinction to be amongst the few folks acknowledged by Sarah Alice Broadbent. She talked to one of the marsh hen hunters from my class one year and to some of the dirty little Caesar children.

When Grandpa tried to survey her land, she shot at his boat. She never did talk to him.

As her property became more valuable, she turned down

offers from Jacksonville developers. Even her relatives tried to get her to sell out.

One night her two-story shingled house burned to the ground. Since she apparently hadn't made it out, the bones they found were sent to the crime lab for examination. It turns out they were not human remains at all. They were animal bones.

Whatever happened to Sarah Alice? We still don't know.

The Blue Seas Café

Every town has a hangout and everyone has a memory of a certain place that signifies the generation. In my little shrimping village hometown there was such a landmark, traditional hangout, and lunchtime spot called the Blue Seas. Lest you begin to think of tiki huts and sarongs, I must tell you that it was not like that. It had a screen door on the south side of the building with a small plywood paneled counter and bar to the left. On the right were about six or seven formica-topped tables in various stages of disrepair that usually had to be balanced by a book of matches or accordion-folded cardboard. A linoleum floor was scrubbed clean but faded from barefooted saltwater visitors.

Later on when the Georgia visitors bought more than grape-flavored snowballs and the folks prospered, a lower level was added on and screened in. The Bowers family, Mr. and Mrs. B plus son Jimmy Bowers, a broad -shouldered football player with a blond crew cut, ran the place. Was there an attractive older sister named Shirley? I think so. If you were on the honor roll or a senior at Fernandina High School, you were allowed forty-five minutes to leave campus at lunchtime. The destination of choice was the Blue Seas or "Bowers" for the ultimate slaw and chili dog plus a fountain coke for fifty cents or $1.25, depending upon the sides you selected.

Outside there was an overhang with three big brown

loudspeakers strategically placed to blast out Pat Boone, Little Richard, or, later in the evening provide music by the Platters for dancing. The sound of "Heavenly shades of night are falling . . ." from the song "Twilight Time" was magically accompanied by the sounds of waves crashing below and the ever constant ocean breeze. Nearby on the bulkhead made of huge rocks, the guys stood in circles and smoked. Once in a while, boys parked in front in trucks with cans of beer displayed on the ends of sunburned arms bronzed from temporary jobs on shrimp boats. Younger boys stood by at the ramp to the beach, waiting to dig out the tires of tourists stuck in the white sand. They happily counted tips from appreciative drivers. A few older men came in for a bite at night to watch the younger crowd and pretend to be young again themselves. Once there was a drowning and I saw my first dead person.

The Blue Seas was a place to show off new sundresses, tans or fresh summer tee shirts and shorts. It was a place to meet up with girlfriends in the winter or to check out the Georgia boys in the summer. It was understood that our local fellows would date Georgia girls in the summer and vice versa and then in September all would be forgiven and we would simply fall into dating each other again. What a wonderful time that was. Such simplicity. Such practicality!

Even today when we hear the words "Blue Seas" or "Bowers" in Fernandina, the older crowd can smell the food and feel the breeze. Our hangout doesn't exist anymore, except in our memories.

GAYLE SWEDMARK HUGHES

The Class of 1957

This class from Fernandina is a very special group. There was no "Beach" in the name in the earlier days. As memorialized by the Statler Brothers song, this bunch comes from the innocent years, at least on the surface. These were the days of manners, minding our parents, and respecting our teachers. It was an era of dressing up for school and even more for church and of walking barefoot when we were not in either place. We were proud of our school and kept it clean. We were not afraid of terrorists. We were more concerned about aliens and we thought that simply getting under our desks would protect us from an atomic attack.

We never locked doors. Neighbors helped neighbors with chores. We delivered big cakes and casseroles to the homes of the bereaved. The only economic fluctuations we knew about were our parents' tales about the Depression and also some layoffs related to the paper mills having shutdowns and a low seafood harvest. The popular Menhaden Fisheries "Pogey" plant that provided oils for cosmetics closed in the 1950s, but otherwise we had a stable economy.

We grew up with harmless pranks like climbing over the fence for a midnight swim in the new city pool, the only one in town. Or calling up stores to ask whether they had "Prince Albert in a can. If you do, you'd better let him out!" we'd say. Much laughter followed by both parties. In our high school years a quarter would get you a gallon of gas, enough to drive around the circle at Moore's at the beach and downtown to the city dock all afternoon.

The girls looked for the Charlotte Hornets baseball players in spring training for the Washington Senators farm club who sat on the porch at the beautiful old Keystone Hotel. The boys looked for Georgia girls.

In the common parlance of the times I was respected but I was popular. In those days dating meant simply going out or hanging around and nothing more. One boy from Georgia, John, was a platonic friend and extremely close to me. We helped each other get through the teen years. He helped me focus on the serious and important things of education and religion. He was a huge intellectual influence. We took turns asking questions of each other from the encyclopedia or college quizzes. He also challenged my mother and, against his parents' wishes, bravely reported to the police that he observed I was being abused. This ended a lot of problems for me. I was, and am, understandably appreciative and we have remained friends all of these years. He has written many books on philosophy and religion, is married to a ballerina. They both prayed for me when, in my sixties, I fought a serious illness. The depth of our friendship is profound. Most of the summer friendships, were, however, superficial and fleeting. But our class stayed close to each other through the winter months, year after year.

This class was, and is, fun-loving. We brought home a huge rock from Natural Bridge, Virginia, from our senior trip to Washington, D.C. It sits in front of the new school with Class of '57 painted on it. We cried at graduation.

Fifty-four years later the class still meets once a month for dinner for those who live in Fernandina and for a major reunion every five years. Our fiftieth reunion was a three-day celebration of a trip to Cumberland Island by boat, a cook-out on the banks of the Bell River and a dance at the club. Today we share our joys and sadness. We dance and party. We attend church. We pray together. We play together. A minister at a funeral held for of one of us last year said, "I have never seen anything like it. This group sitting together today visited their sick and I passed them in the halls of the hospital when I was there." It is indeed a rare, close, and special group. Surely it had something to do with the formation of my personality and life.

Our Last Dock Party

Rain pinged on the tin roof of the old ramshackle Tringalis seafood shed at city dock in Fernandina. As it stopped, the moon lighted our faces. The tide was in. We were looking at the row of fish houses and boat slips on the wharf which had been slowly dwindling as the property got swallowed up for development. The group had gathered to celebrate the view of our beautiful Amelia River, so much a part of the traditional scene. The men were inspired seafood cooks and set out pots of freshly caught treasures on the dock. Women traditionally made a salad and stayed out of the way, dangling feet or leaning against the water-logged posts. It was the first night of our class reunion. In a way we were saying goodbye to a familiar landmark. Our art classes always met in this spot.

One night in the fifties we sat on the dock together and watched the Carnegie Estate, called Dungeness, burn to the ground across the way on Cumberland Island. We thought it was probably torched by a poacher. We thought we knew who it was. Probably someone ejected from the property. Now, after our supper the weather had cleared enough for our night trip to Cumberland Island. George Washington's most brilliant strategist of the American Revolution, General Nathaniel Green, had property there. He spent his own money to feed the hungry troops and buy boots and shoes for the soldiers. The government, as thanks, let his beautiful widow have most of Cumberland Island, before any of the Carnegies staked their claim there. The widow Green entertained both Aaron Burr and Alexander Hamilton there at different times. It has been suggested that the duel that took Hamilton's life was about her. Cumberland has a thousand other stories.

This night, the water lapped against our boat as we approached the mysterious ruins of the burned Carnegie Mansion chimneys silhouetted in the moonlight. Many of the wild horses on the island came to meet us. Night sounds of the birds and critters greeted us and we sang back to them. Old ballads. Our voices blended with the animals of the island. As we returned to the dock at Fernandina at midnight, we saw the signs of construction of three condo units on the wharf. We were all so glad to have had this last trip together before time caught up with us and our landmark was gone forever. That night we talked about graduation week and all of the details that we remembered. We talked about the Sunday when everyone had cried after Baccalaureate. It seems we were reluctant to separate as we walked to our cars on this last dock party night.

Our class had also been reluctant to separate when we were younger and facing being apart. Maybe all classes are. I began to think back to the time of our graduation and the events of those days.

My Mema had come over to stay with us in Fernandina the week of my high school graduation and was amazed at our closeness. She brought her old sewing machine and made three beautiful little shift-style dresses for me to take off to college. She and I walked on the beach and she told me how much it meant to her to have a granddaughter like me. While she was there, I misplaced one of my half slips and Mother was so angry that she refused to talk to me for three days, including graduation day and graduation night. Mema discovered the slip mixed in with her own clothes when she returned home. My mother's demons were strong. I try to convince myself that she was ill and that she actually loved me very much. She may have been jealous of my time and closeness to Mema. She may have thought that I lost the slip in some inappropriate place. She should have not worried. I was a virgin.

College Years

The summer passed. My parents were divorced by now. My dog had died. I can remember approaching the campus of Florida State University in Tallahassee with a sense of wonderment. I was reinforced with the confidence of Anna's admonitions about the Good Lord, the discipline of "Aunt" Ruth's musical classes and Daddy's pride in me. In the distance rose the spires of the Gothic structures of brick all around the circle behind Westcott Fountain. The living space in my freshman dormitory was Spartan at best. There was only an iron bed, a desk with a metal lamp and then the little café curtains and trunk that I added. We were allowed to put photographs, ribbons, and mementoes on the mirror over the chest we shared. The driveway out front was jammed with double-parked parents unloading teddy bears, Lanz dresses and 33 1/3 rpm records from the trunks of cars. There were girls from Miami, from up north, and from other countries—people, it seemed to me, of unimaginable sophistication. It was heady stuff.

The first time I saw O'Joy Lerner I was entranced. She was all of the wild mysterious women of literature: Jade Darnelli, Sadie Thompson, and Ruby Gentry all in one. She wore tight sweaters, had dyed blonde hair with dark roots. She was from Miami! When I first spied her, she was dancing to "Wake up Little Suzie" by the Everly Brothers with a crippled man in the student union at FSU. He looked

61

a lot older. Later he became a prominent stage director. She looked exotic as I sat with the girls from my dorm and stared. We all had on soft leather Capezio flats, white blouses with round collars, circle pins, and ponytails or page boys. We wore Clearasil and Chanel No. 5. O'Joy was from a different planet and we were hypnotized. It has been over fifty years and it is still clear in my mind.

All of us lived in the freshman dorm, Jennie Murphree. We were thinking about the first week of class, rush week at the sororities, and boys. We were "Jennie" girls because we lived in that brick, ivy- covered fortress and the housemother told us that Jennie girls were always little ladies. We were to be in by ten o'clock during the week and eleven o'clock on weekends unless there was a dance. There was one bath area for each of the ten rooms and we had one phone to share at the end of each hallway. Only one girl, Meg, smoked. She had a lighter her boyfriend had given her that she treasured.

The first night we spent in the dorm there was a ruckus. We went out in the hallway in our shorty pajamas where the floor director led a blonde firmly down the corridor. "I am going to report you. I don't care where you are from or who you are! You cannot act like this at FSU. Especially not in Jenny."

Mary Joe, our counselor, was with the floor director. "You have been drinking. Yes, you have! Do you know what time it is?" It was O'Joy and she was an hour past curfew.

"Have you been smoking? You smell like a smokestack!" Mary Joe added. "Peanut butter does not cover the smoke and the alcohol. I still smell you, loud and clear." She told us to get back in our rooms and turn out our lights. It was hard to get back to sleep after learning that the sophisticated woman we had seen in the student union was one of our Jennie girls.

Many more incidents involved O'Joy. We didn't dislike her but we didn't associate with her much either. She walked to class alone with that Marilyn Monroe swing, and at night she usually tried to sneak out to older men. Meg missed her lighter and found it in O'Joy's room. She reported her to the dorm council.

O'Joy went to the infirmary one afternoon and came back crying. Lucy, Sandy, and I tried to talk to her and invited her to go to a movie with us. She just said, "No use," and slammed her door. One night a pale blue Lincoln drove up to Jenny Murphree dorm and O'Joy walked out with an overnight case. A few days later some people came and got her things. We were all simply told that she had left school. The resident director told us she had to. I always wondered if she was pregnant, got caught stealing money, or simply decided she hated us. Maybe we could have been better to her. Maybe we could have helped.

Grades were not wonderful and I had to get a tutor one year for physics. Our high school had been strong in the humanities but notoriously weak in science. I didn't settle down until my second year. I was active in the sorority and, unfortunately, a leader of pranks. One significant event comes to mind.

It wasn't vandalism and it wasn't illegal. It wasn't even destruction of property because it was understood by both parties that it was going to happen. In a tradition as old as the college and a part of its lore, the fraternities tried to protect their symbols and the sororities tried to get to them and conquer. For the S.A.E.'s (Sigma Alpha Epsilon) that proud symbol was the Lion. It stood in front of their house on Tennessee Street and was guarded during rush week by pledges who slept outside every night. It seems silly and juvenile now. Then, it was a time of earnest effort. During the era of Soap Box Derby down College Avenue and intramural games, it was normal. Attacks were expected and the challenge was welcomed. The Lion was covered in a polyurethane substance to make it impervious to paints. Dousing it in paint was the object. It was good fun. Usually. The penalty for getting caught was the shaving of the head of the offender.

As a new pledge, the youngest member of my class, I was dauntless. Having dual-enrolled at fifteen with college status, I was now ensconced permanently on campus as a resident and still only sixteen. I was so young. Also stupid. I was assigned by my elders to paint the S.A.E. Lion. At night. Alone. It was the week before the Homecoming celebration.

In black bermuda shorts, tennis shoes with soft soles, and a plain black tee shirt, I set out to conquer the symbol of Sigma Alpha Epsilon. It was scary enough approaching in the dark, but I was in luck when I saw two of their pledges stretched out on the lawn sound asleep. Another was stationed at the steps of the house, reading a textbook under the porch light. With the stealth of a Green Beret, I approached the end of the house and ran quickly to the Lion with a paper cup full of pink paint. (Pink to let them know who claimed the deed and further assault their masculine senses).

Splat! *Well done!* I thought. Off I ran towards the road to catch a ride from my waiting sisters. With the young strong knees of youth, I ran like the wind, easily outpacing the awakening young pledges and the boy coming from the steps. One. Two. Three. Almost there! Whoop, a hairy hand gripped my right ankle. It was another S.A.E. who had come unseen from the other side of the house to greet me. Down we went in a tangle. Soon lights went on in the house and I heard the buzz of clippers coming towards me.

Hugh Wilson, a pal from Lake City, said, "Don't cut her hair!"

Someone else said, "She should have thought about that before she came over here to torment our beast!"

My skin itched where the razor mowed down brown ringlets. I heard Colin Phipps or Bill Grow say, "Stop." The others agreed. "We'll let you go with just half of it shaved."

At the Homecoming dance, I was the one with the silk scarf draped across her face and the gold hoop earring. One earring. It stayed on almost the whole night. My date was furious with the boys who had shaved my head. Several of them asked me to dance in sympathy.

There were so many characters to meet in college. There was the big guy named Benny from Wewahitchka with the pink Cadillac convertible who sold Goodie Headache Powders and kept his phone book in the refrigerator so he could always find it. There was Tookie Mixon who raised ornamental cabbages on the walkway to his fraternity house and ran for class president with the slogan "Homegrown is best." There was a guy from Ft. Walton Beach who was afraid of spiders and jumped up in my lap at a football game when he saw one. There were so many unusual people. Of all the boys I think of now, and certainly not in a romantic way, I wonder most about Zero. I don't know his real name, but he got the nickname because he was said to have no money, no looks, no personality. Another person said it was because he got zero strikes at bat in the championship game for his hometown in Georgia, some small place near Bainbridge or Cairo.

Zero was not in a fraternity. He was never known to have dated. He was a student lab assistant and smart as a whip in the sciences. Daddy hired him to tutor me in physics and organic chemistry, which were about to drag my grade point down. It just so happened that I was going through my anti-snobbery phase. One night at the sorority house, talk turned to the upcoming Rose Weekend which was our spring formal event. The girls said, "You're going to bring Joe, right?" That would add to our prestige since Joe was a football player and well known. I had been dating him some. In a moment of contrariness I blurted out, "No, I am asking Zero Wallslager." Shock. Next, I had to explain to Joe why I wasn't asking him to our sorority's most important dance of the year. Then I had to ask Zero. It was too late to back down. I caught him after lab and he said yes. I was to be his first date at FSU.

At the dance at the Old Floridan Hotel on Monroe

Street, Zero was attentive enough to ask me if I wanted punch. I said, "Sure," and off he went, returning just as the band launched into the "Dream Man Song." At this point in the evening the favorite man in all the world of our club was to walk under the trellis arches of paper rosebuds and we were all to rise in our pink formals and sing. Zero took a shortcut to avoid walking in front of the band. He stepped through the arch with a giant smile just as the theme began to crescendo. A roar went up, and the guy trailing behind him was ignored. Zero's picture was on the front page of our school paper, the *Flambeau*, on Monday. The next week he was the hit of the campus. Last I heard, he was invited to dinner at the Pi Phi house, the Chi Omega house, and so on. Wonder what ever happened to him?

A National Convention

As a teenager I wasn't very political. The first political show I saw was the one that nominated Eisenhower over Taft, the first televised convention. In the summer of my college years, I was visiting Mama and her second husband, Les Robinson, in New York City. I met a neighbor named Marian and she took me to a little studio to watch the taping of a television show called "*Who Do You Trust?*" She was a guest contestant on the show and the host was a skinny guy named Johnny Carson.

While I was waiting for her, a man came up to me and asked me if I wanted to be one of the Nixon girls at the National Convention that summer. I had no idea what that meant but said I would explore the possibility of doing it. Soon I was being fitted with dresses in blue and white fabric with NIXON imprinted all over the material. I know. It sounds tacky. It was.

I went with nine other young women on a nice bus to Chicago to the 1960 Republican National Convention where we were given rooms at the Conrad Hilton Hotel, wonderful meals, and a chaperone. I was sent off to the airport one morning to greet folks getting off the planes. With me stood a man in Abraham Lincoln costume with a beard. One afternoon two of us were able to sit up front in the seat on the Budweiser-Clydesdale wagon and were pulled right down Michigan Avenue. We chanted "Nixon and the

Sox! Nixon and the Sox!" The Chicago White Sox were a hometown favorite.

In the days before the fax machine and other electronic marvels, we hand-carried speeches to the delegates and guests after corrections or additions were made in the typing pool. I recall getting into a taxi cab and taking a revised speech to Senator Walter Judd, who was making the keynote address. He was polite and his staff invited me to have a sandwich in the hospitality room. Once Barry Goldwater from Arizona sent a few buckets of chicken over to our lounge area. Our supervisor in Chicago was a man named Harry Robbins Haldeman, later the Bob Haldeman of Watergate fame.

We were introduced to Nixon, but he seemed preoccupied and looked past us as we spoke. More overwhelming was my brief moment to shake President Eisenhower's hand. His open car had cut away from the parade as it finished, and I was walking across the street at the time with my Nixon dress on. I went over to his open car and stuck my hand in. All I could think of to say in the face of that fatherly grin was, "God Bless you, Mr. President." He shook my hand and his car pulled away, leaving me standing there in the street with my mouth open. It was a memorable experience for a young woman from a small town in north Florida.

Meeting people made me serious about school. Many of the young people with whom I worked in Chicago were going to graduate school, some to law school.

Once I adjusted to the independent atmosphere, my grades took a climb and my intellectual curiosity caught fire.

TWO THOUSAND DAFFODILS

By my junior year I was beginning to have higher ambitions and think of graduate school. At that time I was about to have a new experience in a distant part of the country.

Washington State

In the early days of my junior year at FSU, Daddy called to say that his paper company needed him to take over in Port Angeles, Washington. On the map it appeared to be as far away as possible from north Florida and still be within the continental states. Some three thousand miles. My precious grandmother moved with us and I was to find a place for her and for Daddy to live and set up housekeeping together. What a new experience it turned out to be. The Northwest was majestic, the life style was casual, and I made some friends who are still close to this day. I found us a pretty cedar-shake shingled house, U-shaped with a courtyard of saucer-sized geraniums. The house sat on a high bluff overlooking the Straits of Juan de Fuca. A German range finder was installed on the kitchen breakfast nook so Gammy could see the ships coming into the harbor. She had a constantly changing scene to entertain her. Each morning she would say, "Dear, you just must come see this wonderful sight" and point to some Japanese ship or other vessel. Never have I seen a woman give up a home where she lived for sixty years and move away as graciously as she did. Being with us made it bearable for her, and the tears she must have shed fell while she was alone. On the flight west she smiled at me and as she sipped her first glass of champagne, said, "Here begins a new chapter!"

I held her little hand on take-off and we smiled hopefully

at each other. Though feeling far away from all of my friends and leaving the soft security of live oaks and crepe myrtles of north Florida, I soon was seduced by the glorious beauty of the evergreens and mountains. In our living room you could sit in one chair and see the water of the straits down below us to the north and the white tops of the Hurricane Ridge on the Olympic mountain range to the south. Heady stuff for me. I explored the rain forest, discovered new berries, and ate salmon for the first time. I got the house organized and cooked. I took Gammy to the Seattle World's Fair on her eightieth birthday. We had lunch in the Space Needle. Gammy soon made friends with neighbors and church members out in Washington State and Daddy joined a wonderful foursome for golf every Saturday at the Olympic Country Club.

One Saturday while Daddy was golfing with his foursome, I was in the passenger seat of a new 1959 Ford Wagon climbing up the eleven-mile winding road to Hurricane Ridge, visible from our own living room in Port Angeles. The sky was cloudless and the air crystal clear. Driving was thirty-one year old Bill Fairchild, company pilot for the paper company, a man with a killer smile, lake blue eyes and a head full of neatly trimmed black curls. He wore aviator sunglasses and a flight jacket. As a nineteen-year-old college student, I found him as irresistible as Smilin' Jack in the comics. He was polite and deferential to me as the boss's daughter. He may have had an idea that I had a crush on him but he was careful not to encourage that.

On the Thursday before, when I had picked Daddy up

at the private airport, Bill had asked me if I wanted to go flying sometime. He had heard from Daddy that I wanted to take lessons.

"Sure," I said. If he had suggested that we jump off the top of the mountain into a kiddy pool I would have said "sure."

As they tied down the plane, Daddy said, " Bill is safety conscious, Princess, and he has a chance to fly off the top of Hurricane Ridge. He will have to drop a little bit before the plane actually picks up the airspeed it needs since there is no runway. Do you think you can handle that?" It seemed easy at the time, a wonderful opportunity.

I had seen the top of beautiful Hurricane Ridge, 7,900 plus feet above our home. It looked benign and heavenly. You could see the lights of Parliament in Victoria, British Columbia, across the water from our house and the snow on the ridge on the American side. It seemed safe. As we wound our way up to the peak, fear gripped me. I was never even particularly good on roller coasters. I found myself hoping for an appendicitis attack or maybe a car crash and I could just be in the hospital for a few months. Had I remembered to tell Gammy that I loved her?

"Ready?" Bill said.

"Sure," I answered and hopped out of the station wagon and into the airplane with a hand held by Bill to steady me. I gulped, strapped on the belt, and heard the purring of the Pratt and Whitney engine warming up and then we dropped into a free fall off the cliff. Finally I heard the sweet, sweet sound of the power building and the plane climbed.

Hallelujah!

Eleven years later I became a pilot. The same year Bill Fairchild was killed on a routine flight to Seattle on a clear day. The engine failed.

Living Large at the Doric Bellingham Hotel

When the state of Washington needed dormitory space in a hurry, it leased commercial space, including two floors in the old hotel where I found myself scheduled to room with Janie Jansen. I was attending Western Washington University with girls from Oregon, Hawaii, and California. We were excited to move in.

The Doric Bellingham Hotel was not the grande dame she had been in her glory days of the 1950s, but she had her charms. Chief of these was the beautiful Florentine Room, a rooftop restaurant with a view of Mt. Baker. Also, as you entered the front lobby, you passed the lively San Juan Bar on the left and an attractive ski mural featuring Mount Baker on the right. The Bon Marché Department Store was across the street.

Though poor college students we were, ambience was important to lovely Janie and also to me. We selected framed prints from the Chatham County Library to be replaced each month at no cost. We pinned our best silk scarves around the pillows in our room to add cheer to the surroundings. We set out a large Schefflera tree borrowed from Janie's dad's florist business.

Hans, the chef at the hotel, was enchanted with Janie and saved all of the hors d'oeuvres from parties in the Florentine Room to donate to our tiny fridge. Sometimes we had caviar or pate for breakfast. Axel, the day desk clerk, was

75

inclined to notice me and so our messages received V.I.P. treatment and were delivered promptly to our room with a flourish in a white and gold hotel envelope. He had our class schedule and called us to be sure we were up.

Janie turned out to be a dream roommate and an even better friend who would make my bed to surprise me when I rushed off to an exam or left before she did. Now Jane Jansen Jobe, she has been a lifelong friend. She and her husband Tom came from Seattle to our youngest son Lance's wedding in 2000 at Pebble Hill Plantation in Thomasville, Georgia. We celebrated our birthdays together and her successful bone marrow transplant ten years ago was joyfully acknowledged by a joint trip to the Biltmore Hotel in Asheville, N.C. We sat on top of the mountain and sang "Great is Thy Faithfulness."

We agree that, even at the peak of our careers in later life, we never lived any better than we did at the old Doric Bellingham Hotel.

Social Life in the Great Northwest

The group of folks I met at Western Washington University were more athletic than I. They hiked, explored, fished, whale-watched, and played rugby. They welcomed me, liked my Southern accent, and included me in most of their activities.

The dating pattern then out on the west coast of Canada and U.S. centered around group activities and sports. No pairing off of couples until folks got very serious. So, it was all of us, in a group, heading to Shakey's Pizza Parlor for banjo music or to the Purple Onion for comedy. Mostly, though, it was all about the outdoors. I went with the Burton brothers, Ken and Ron, to a wiener roast at the narrow beach on Chuckanut Drive. We climbed down a very steep incline to a small strip on the water for our cookout. This is a twenty-one mile scenic route of high, rough coastal highway. The climb back up would be on a tiny trail known as Deception Pass, a passage both treacherous and beautiful.

Crushed clamshells serve as sand to make the beautiful white beaches of Teddy Bear Cove. About twelve of us settled down to tell stories and sing after supper. Gradually folks began drifting home. Ken and Ron agreed to put out the fire. We told some more ghost stories and suddenly the sky turned to indigo. The climb back up was on a barely visible tiny trail. The guys, being extremely athletic, did not seem worried. I was.

Not only was it dark, but the water crept closer and closer as we packed up our gear. Soon the water was up to the rock cliff and our ankles were under water. Next it was a matter of clawing our way up rough vegetation, rocks and vines, to try to get up the cliff and out of the water. It became pitch dark. As I recall it today, I vividly remember Ron sliding back down the cliff some fifteen feet or so. Four and a half hours later we made it to the top of the cliff onto the road. We were nowhere near our car but flagged down a motorist to take us back to Bellingham. When I got to the door of my place, I must have been a sight, because my hair was tangled, my shirt torn and muddy, and my tennis shoes were cut. My roommate nearly fainted, I think. Wow. Now I watch water levels and daylight much better. I think I know what they meant by Deception Pass.

After I left the West, for a while I went to New York City to visit my mother and get a taste of metropolitan life. It was a pivotal time and a turning point in my life.

He Came To See My Boss

This is a story I wanted to tell my son. I was working in New York City, single and not yet in law school. I lived with my mother and stepfather in a very nice apartment paid for by them. I had obtained a summer job as a lowly clerk at J. Walter Thompson advertising agency. If there was a spot on the pecking order below mine, I was not aware of it. I was temporarily assigned to a political client with a small office on 42nd Street. My wardrobe consisted of a few paisley wrap dresses and two nice quality shirtwaist dresses, but I was also able to raid my mother's closets for great outfits from Peck & Peck and Lord & Taylor. I was a size six with shoulder length brown hair and a nice summer tan.

One day I was assigned to the sophisticated Mark McCabe, a V.P., while his secretary was out. So conscientious was I that I stayed at my desk through most of lunch to catch up. A stocky man with piercing dark eyes came in and asked to see Mr. McCabe. I thought he said his name was Dr. Brown, but I wasn't sure. Explaining that my boss would be back in a half hour, I invited him to wait or to go next door to Schrafft's on 42nd St. with me to have a quick bite at the counter. He accepted and as we walked out the door to a summer heat wave he opened the door ahead of me and guided me with his hand.

We talked at lunch about religion, music, politics, and marriage. He told me that he was pleased with his marriage but that so many people were not. He just had a new baby, as I recall, a little girl. He felt too many people were not settled. He asked me about my childhood and future plans. He said that his childhood in Germany was much like mine. I doubted that. When we returned to the office, Mr. McCabe was there and they closed the door of the inner office for the remainder of the afternoon. Later that day my boss told me that the visitor had thought I was a bright young lady. I told him that I was completely enchanted with the doctor and that he seemed really, really smart. Mark McCabe laughed and said, "You know he is the father of the rocket. The heart of our space program."

McCabe, who lived in the suburbs, invited me to dinner with the two of them and I said, "Why don't you come over to the apartment and I will cook?" Actually I already had spaghetti and meatballs done. My parents' Park Avenue apartment was less than five blocks away at 37th Street. The irony of serving spaghetti to a distinguished German was lost on me. Making a salad with the help of the guests, I apologized for the menu. They both said that it sounded great. We ate and talked for two hours over the nice red wine purloined from my stepfather's cabinet. I explained that they were in London. To say that I was delighted would be an understatement. At the door as they left my boss said, "See you tomorrow. It was great."

The guest gave me a brotherly hug and said, "I will keep track of you." In a daze, with the glow of the evening, I cleaned up the kitchen while opera music blared from next door.

GAYLE SWEDMARK HUGHES

Only a few years later Mrs. James Van Allen, my next door neighbor in Iowa City, told me they were having very distinguished company, Dr. Von Breun, and that she wanted me and my husband to come to dinner so that I could help her entertain, cook, and also give moral support. She had taught me how to make bread. Her husband was the scientist who discovered the Van Allen Radiation Belts around the Earth. When the night arrived, I wore my best dress and did my hair right, wanting to impress. I knew Dr. Von Breun probably wouldn't remember me, but as he walked into the dining room he said, "Gayle, how nice to see you again. I hear you are quite the star at the law school." I was thrilled.

Another few years passed by and one night when visiting my hometown and driving around the golf course, I heard on the car radio that Dr. Wernher von Breun had died. I pulled over and said a little quiet prayer.

An Angel on the Streets of New York

The first time I saw Rosie she was sitting on the curb at 42nd Street in her ugly scuffed brown shoes and white socks and her felt cap and wormy sweater. She smelled good though, or at least she didn't smell bad. She bathed at the nearby Episcopal Center where she ate her meals. She minded their rules. She had to bathe to eat there and so she did. She was hungry and a pragmatist. Made sense to me.

The first few days that I noticed her she was mumbling or talking to strangers and one day she yelled, "WIDE IS THE GATE THAT LEADS TO TEMPTATION!"

I self-consciously said to my lunch companion, "She *knows* me," and we laughed sort of smugly. By then I was sure that Rosie was certifiable.

Soon enough I was to become better acquainted when I saw Rosie talking with a well-dressed "Lady Bountiful" type she introduced to me as Jane. *Well, okay,* I thought, *since Jane talks to her, I might as well.* Rosie needed a good meal so I eventually took her to my mother's Park Avenue apartment nearby and we enjoyed lamb chops and looking out at the street from the communal roof garden on top of the building. She assured me that she knew Nelson Rockefeller and others of prominence.

Sure, right, I'll bet, I thought. One night Rosie and I were on the way to the movies at Grand Central Station and passed a political rally featuring a smiling Nelson Rockefeller.

Gayle Swedmark and Frank Hughes as children

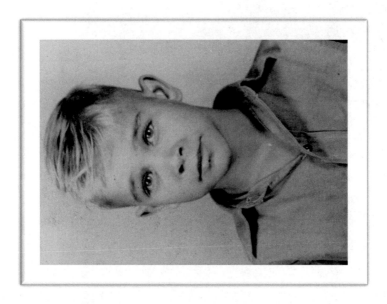

Gayle as a fifteen year old

Gayle and son Lance

Salem Black River
Church where Matthew
Peterson Mayes was an
Elder.

Thomas Alexander Mayes Home

Daddy and Lance at graduation

Lance and Jennifer whale watching

Ophelia on her 80th birthday
Photo by Frank Hughes

Gayle with Ed Asner

Frank in later years

Amelia Island beach scene
Photo by Frank Hughes

Nixon and Lodge banner and the Nixon girls

Frank and Gayle at the Peanut Festival in 2010

The glass prism from Anna

Oxford University (View from Gayle's window; street scene)

He yelled out, "Hey Rosie! How ya doin'?" Was I ever surprised!

Rosie was concerned about the poor people and kept after leaders in public life to do more. She got me to help her with some minor missions. I got to know her friend, the Episcopal Jane, better. When Jane found out that I was bound for law school in Iowa, she had quite a surprise for me. She owned a house there, tied up in a complicated trust so that she could not sell it, but could simply use it in her lifetime for herself or her friends. It had been left to her by one of her late husbands. She had no interest in moving to the Midwest. I became the beneficiary of all this. Even now I find it a miracle. For three wonderful years, paying only utilities and telephone, I lived in a house on beautiful Summit Street with china service for twenty-four, a library with a heavy oak pocket door, and my own asparagus bed. Rosie sure knew how to network.

It became apparent that Rosie knew a lot of things. She counseled me on life and the mysteries of the universe. She had pride that belied her station in life. She had dignity and faith. She was, to me, a glimpse of an angel on the streets of New York City.

The House on Summit Street

Some of my friends thought I would be culturally deprived moving to the Midwest and out of the mainstream. Someone needed to tell them that Iowa had the highest literacy rate in the country that year. The whole experience turned out to be a fortunate choice for graduate school and a totally wonderful time of my school life. I will never completely understand what forces led me to Rosie in New York, thereby to her friend Jane and the gift of her house.

The house I moved into was a magical turn-of-the-century place. It had three stories and a wrap-around porch. Blue Venetian glass lit the entry and solid wood pocket doors led to the library. The side yard had lots of peonies and lilacs for this Southerner to admire and pick. The windows could be open in the fall and I could look from my upstairs bedroom down a wide tree-lined street with wonderful sidewalks. My S and H green stamp lamps seemed perfectly at home with the gorgeous carpets of the bedrooms.

Across the street was Forest Evashevski, athletic director and former Big Ten coach, who coached Iowa to two Rose Bowl Titles. He had blocked for Tom Harmon at Michigan. His son played for Michigan the year we moved to Summit Street. Next door to them was the wonderful Van Allen house. Dr. James Van Allen was a space scientist who headed up the physics department at the University of Iowa when we moved to town.

GAYLE SWEDMARK HUGHES

On my north side was the Mauricio Lasansky home. An American graphic artist and printmaker he is called one of the "Fathers of 20th Century American Printmaking." He established a workshop at the Iowa School of Art and Art History that is a model for other universities. He wasn't friendly and seemed irritated to have other people in his space. Still, I knew there were some artistic vibrations in the air and it made the street seem cosmopolitan and sophisticated. On my left side was Jessie Gordon, a bookstore owner, we would have once called an "old maid," who lived in the old Grant Wood home. It was a two-story frame house and soon she took me under her protective wing. Her tenants, who were in the famed University of Iowa Writers Workshop, taught me a lot about cooking. They laughed at me for being too eager to please others and they taught me to be a little more direct and assertive. What a neighborhood! I found new authors to read, new recipes to try and a whole lot of education still to be absorbed.

Law School Is Not for Sissies

Though not the first woman to enter University of Iowa School of Law, I was the only one in my class at the time I began. It felt awkward, and an awesome task to try to trail blaze. For women coming after me, I did feel some obligation not to fail. The first class day as I entered the amphitheater for Freshman Procedure class with the intimidating professor Allan Vestal, feet scraped and shuffled against the floor to signify disapproval. Well, what must I do? Surely my face was pink! I almost stumbled on the first step up to the amphitheater. Though I nearly burst into tears of frustration, I knew that would be the worst possible thing.

Instead I stepped backward, turned toward the professor, and then walked over in front of him to the center of the room and faced the class. There I shuffled my feet myself, doing a quick tap dance step, an awkward twirl, and an elaborate bow. Amazingly, there was a spattering of applause and then some more. Finally, at Professor Vestal's signal, the class stood to acknowledge the new member of the group. Thankfully, I became a true pal to many and later a member of the board of editors of law review.

It would be wonderful to say that it was all smooth after the first day, but the truth is there were a few more mean practical jokes and some vicious rumors, though not generally from the folks who lasted the whole three years of law school. On the funny side, there was no student restroom for women in the new law building. To use the secretaries' "staff" room, I had to climb three flights of stairs and go to the opposite end of the hall. To solve this, I constructed a cardboard reversible sign to attach to one of the necessary rooms in an obscure part of the basement much nearer to our classrooms. I also added several pots of ivy in certain places. I did not, as it is now told, put pink ribbons on the plants.

Charlie Milton, a classmate, called in the late 1990s asking me to suggest a Tampa attorney on a case he had, and he told me that he thought of me when he took his granddaughter to law school. He noted there were more than fifty percent women in her class. He said he told her about one woman who almost got shuffled out of freshman class and later became his good friend and colleague.

I made friends with some of the wives and we visited in each other's homes. When they came to visit their husbands on campus, they made time for coffee with me. Some were friendly. Some were not. Stephanie, wife of one of the law students who studied with me, was one of my favorites and she was glad to have me nearby one winter day. Seven months pregnant, she was climbing the two long flights of outdoor stairs up to the student commons with me. The climb was made more treacherous by ice covering the steps. I was one step behind her that morning. We were half way up when she slipped back, landing on top of me. I was wrapped in my trademark outfit, an old raccoon coat that had been a gift. I tucked my arms around Stephanie, hugging her to me. We both slid the length of the staircase. Professor Davidson watched in shock. A quick check at the hospital for her and we had good news: no harm was done.

Living in the house on Summit Street was a huge blessing, but law school remained a difficult track to follow. I had three part time jobs. By the end of my freshman year, I was stressed to the limit emotionally because I knew that I was a role model and a sort of standard bearer and that I was being watched by faculty as well as fellow students. I set high standards for myself and tried much too hard to be Superwoman. I needed sleep. By the time I was a junior, I was getting superior grades, cooking meals every night and even making my own catsup. I cleaned house. I entertained family. I was tired. I was anxious about the future. I never had time to read a book or to go to a movie. I didn't have enough cash to buy a new pair of sneakers. One day I sat on a bench in downtown Iowa City and just cried my heart out. If I were there today I would relax a little and settle for medium grades. I just didn't want to let anyone down. Daddy, it can be said, was a proud father on graduation day and flew from Washington State to attend the ceremony.

The Job Hunt

It was time to search for a paying job. My spouse had his doctorate in hand by then. In those days, it fell my lot to wait until he found a job and then start looking for something for me to do. It did not occur to me to complain. That is simply the way it was at that time. Fortunately for me, he took a position on the faculty at Florida State University in Tallahassee, Florida. It was hard to disguise my happiness in returning to a town I had always loved. It was also fun to give away most of my snow clothes.

As soon as I had unpacked and found a rental house for us in a cheap section of town, I put on my best navy blue suit. Actually it was my only suit. I naively went straight up to the Supreme Court Building and marched to the door of the chief justice. It is crazy now to think that would work in the job search.

Miraculously, right away, I met Millard Caldwell. He was the chief justice of the Florida Supreme Court. He looked it. Tall, gray-haired and handsome, he was straight out of central casting for that part. There will be more about him later, but at this first meeting I knew he was the man to help me. His office had a leathery scent and a male feel. Even the art was masculine. The carpet was steel gray and thick. Both the door to the hallway and the one to his inner office were wide open. It was my good fortune that his staff was at lunch and he waved me in.

He invited me to sit before I could get out my name.

"I need a job," I said.

He smiled pleasantly but not derisively when I told him I had not taken and passed the Florida Bar examination yet and that I had no experience. I put my law school record on his beautiful cherry desk. He examined it carefully and noted that I was at the University of Iowa when President Kennedy was shot. He expressed his disgust that such a bright young man was stricken down and he said we all remember where we were that day. He said that he had worked for President Truman once.

"Well," he said, thoughtfully, as he rose, "I think Wallace Sturgis needs a law clerk." He walked to the other phone extension and asked the operator to get him the First District Court of Appeals, chief judge's office. "Wallace," he said when the judge came on the line, "I have this pretty young girl who was on the law review at University of Iowa, but she's from over there in Fernandina where our friend Tom Shave practices law. You can give him a call about her. Check her out. I do think it is time for you to consider hiring a female and this seems like a good one." He told him I would be down shortly.

When I entered the office, some older men were planning a gin rummy game. The men gallantly stood, even though they all outranked me in every respect. Three of them interviewed me on the spot. I now know that they were all judges on the court.

Judge Carroll spoke first. "Hey there, young lady. So you want to try to get into this law business, do you? Are you married? Do you plan to have children? How would you feel if your husband complained about your working late?"

Before I could answer, Judge Sturgis interjected. "Now, now," he said. "When have we ever worked late?" Laughs all around.

Judge Sturgis continued. "Are you going to get your feelings hurt if I ask you to hand me a cup of coffee when I am on the phone or would you be willing to do that on a rare occasion?"

"I will, if you will," I said. More laughs all around again.

Judge John Wigginton said, "If I gave you an opinion to write and told you what to say, but you disagreed with me, what would you do?"

"I would look at the name and title on your desk, Your Honor. I am merely the scrivener. You are always the judge."

I got the job. Judge Sturgis was a mountain of a man who had been president of the Florida Senate. He was a Mississippi gentleman who called me "Sugah." By today's standards that is wrong, but he always treated me with respect and kindness.

It was a gorgeous office in the Supreme Court Building at that time and I loved being surrounded by marble and by libraries. It was heaven. We had a chance to sit in and listen to major cases being argued. The judges treated us like family and we sent out to the State Bakery for sandwiches on rainy days and ate together with the court.

I now had time, finally, to do a lot of things that there was either not money or time for in law school. I had postponed my desire to fly an airplane for both of those reasons. Now I had the time. I wanted to take the plunge and learn to do it.

A First Solo

Next to falling in love and having a baby, my first solo was the greatest experience of my life. It was in a little blue Cessna with the call signals 4 LY14, which was referred to as Four Lima Yankee. The L stands for Lima and the Y stands for Yankee in aviator's alphabet, similar to the military one.

My flight instructor, Dale Sauers, Jr., had hinted that I should wear old clothes to the lesson on that cold Thursday afternoon. It is traditional to cut the pilot's shirt off to signify a first solo so that people in the terminal know what has just happened. It is a proud moment, of course. I was, therefore, suspicious that I would be ready to solo soon. I had enough hours to solo. But when we finished pre-flighting the airplane, Dale got in with me as usual and off we flew together to practice touch and go's, which are, in effect, takeoffs and landings. I was so surprised when on the third go round he got out and said, "Take it up." Whew! My palms were wet, my throat dry. But I felt joyous. I had beaten gravity. I could see the state capitol building off my right wing. I felt like a helium balloon climbing and climbing up. My instructor weighed 230 pounds and so when he got out of the 1,300 pound airplane it was remarkably light and had much more lift. All I could think of was the phrase, "The unbearable lightness of being," as I heard the tower say, "Four Lima Yankee, (oops that's me!) turn two seven zero. Traffic on approach." The rest of it is a blur to me except that there were sea gulls to follow and some colorful sky divers in parachutes near Lake Talquin.

Soon it was over and I lined up to land on runway 27. After I executed a smooth landing, the tower told me to taxi to the ramp. As I climbed out of 4 Lima Yankee and tied down, my teacher was standing at the door of General Aviation smiling broadly. The whole crew and fuel staff came running with scissors.

Dale yelled, " You *cannot* cut her shirt in the front." They didn't. They took a nice section out of the back and I went proudly with them dressed that way to buy the traditional beer at the main terminal. Another layer of fear peeled back. I was indeed, that day, the Good Lord's happy child.

A Member of the Florida Bar

After I passed the Florida Bar Exam, I went to the old Road Department, now Department of Transportation for trial experience. They let me try cases from the first week. After a confrontation Leo Foster hired me to go with his firm, Parker, Foster, and Madigan, in private practice.

It was only after I was hired that I told the partners of an earlier connection I had with the firm. I applied to them while in law school and had correspondence with the then senior partner, Julius F. Parker, Sr. We wrote back and forth and he suggested some courses that would be appropriate if I went to work for that firm. He told me what type of clients they had and said that he would give me a chance to work for them, subject to an interview and background check. He said, "Come on over to the office as soon as you get here." He died before I moved. It was either on the way to or home from the Kentucky Derby. I got to Tallahassee the next week. I did not think it proper to trade on a deceased partner's tentative promise. I didn't call them. Now I was hired at the firm that had been my first choice and that I had contacted earlier.

By the time I was twenty-seven, I was a named partner in the firm now called Madigan, Parker, Gatlin and Swedmark. The career brought me in contact with the finest and the worst of mankind. I arranged a lovely office with my crystal glass paperweight from Anna on the left of my desk to remind me of her words to me.

Early in my career I learned that if I was going to represent sheriffs, as the firm currently did, I could not be faint hearted. One of the earliest parties I attended was a wild game feast hosted by Sheriff John Whitehead of Union County, Florida. He was an adorable man, friendly to all and the president of the Florida Sheriffs Association. When I arrived at his farm, not a woman in sight, he walked away from some cabinet members and came to greet me genially. He took my jacket and I thought how nice that was. Soon I heard some hounds baying. They came swarming around me. Cornered, I jumped up on the nearest picnic table, ice tea jug and all. Everyone laughed. I managed a weak laugh. The dogs stood around the table, looking up at me and Sheriff Whitehead called them off. Jack Madigan, my law partner, said, "John, you could have scared her to death. She could have been hurt!"

"Shoot, Jack. I was just training these new dogs to use over at the prison. I wanted to see how they would do with a new scent."

"Never mind, John. She likes dogs and she seems to be handling your sense of humor fairly well."

"Sorry, Miss Gayle. I just wanted to see if you were a good sport. You're all right. You know that? I think you're gonna be just fine. Yes sirree." Later, in cases where I represented Sheriff John Whitehead, he was the model client. He was intelligent and gave me a great deal of respect when I made suggestions to him or explained the law. He treated me as an equal. Those who are old enough remember my introduction to the sheriffs' group and their sense of humor. I managed to enjoy them and tried to fit in over the decades of doing their legal work. I also gently chided them to new and modern ways. I encouraged my partners as well to think in terms of the new rules about women and to lose some of their old habits and expressions. My partners were completely open to women in business and to broad-minded attitudes about women in the profession in general. Still, old habits were hard to break.

In Washington, D.C., one time I attended a fairly posh party with one of my law partners, Jack Madigan, who was the sweetest, most fair guy on earth. Still he had some old-fashioned ways he didn't even realize he had. He was fond of saying, "Who do you belong to?" when he met a pretty lady at a cocktail party. I had already preached to him about that. This particular night a woman actually approached him first with hand extended and he graciously greeted her and said, nervously, "Who do you belong to?"

I was standing at his side when she said, "My name is Dixie Lee Ray. I am chairman of the Atomic Energy Commission!" It was a priceless moment and he learned his lesson. I was too sympathetic to rub it in. You simply had to keep your sense of humor with this business and with these men. However, my sense of humor sometimes got me in trouble.

One time in a relatively minor matter down in Wakulla County, the day was dragging on in tedious testimony full of lies. A witness had spent at least two hours lying. The court knew it. The jury knew it. I knew it. I had just about enough of it. In my cross-examination, instead of using the customary admonition and reminding him of the penalty for perjury, I followed my instinct. I approached him slowly and quietly and said, "Did you know, sir, that if you tell a lie you will get a bump on the end of your tongue?" I pointed to the very tip of my own tongue. "Right there," I said. The jury howled in laughter. Judge Taylor reacted quickly, as he should have. The ghost of a smile passed over his chalk-line mouth. He thought it was funny. I know he did. But he did his duty and in a masterful voice he chided me. "Counsel, you will please approach the bench!" He reprimanded me. He had to. It was worth it. What a day!

Sometimes I had assignments that were not fun. I would find myself driving the Interstate to a hearing in some small town when I had the flu or flying off to some place in South Florida and missing the next flight due to weather. Car trips could go late in the night after a trial or early in the dark morning for a trip for a deposition. In the car I carried a large woven basket with home baked goodies and medicines and other essentials for road trips with young associates. Laurie Beth Woodham, now attorney for the city of Tampa, named it my Mary Poppins bag and it is remembered by many a north Florida lawyer who worked with our firm. I even carried bandages for cuts and phone numbers for emergency car problems. Whether by air or land there were long days. Trying times. It wasn't all glamorous. That is for sure. One such time is particularly vivid to me.

It was a hot and dusty day in Sarasota County as I entered the barbed wire area of the correctional facility. My

6 a.m. flight out of Tallahassee had arrived in Tampa International on time and after maneuvering through the rental car process I was on the way through big city work traffic, and eventually on down the Interstate south to my exit in Sarasota.

Judge John Moore, a federal judge in Jacksonville, had ordered me to meet with Mr. Tyrone Sanson, who was a convicted rapist and murderer. I represented Scott Lancaster, Sheriff of Clay County, Florida, whom Tyrone was suing. The judge made me meet in person to finalize pretrial documents, and since Tyrone obviously couldn't come to me I was required to go to him. My motion to accomplish this project by telephone had been denied by a magistrate without going to the judge.

Now, as I passed through security, got my badge, gave up my earrings and drivers license and bar card, I walked into a sandy yard and looked for the staff member who had agreed to accompany me as protection. A sloppy looking correctional officer approached and said, "We can't spare anyone today. Come back another day if you have a problem with that." He walked away. I had already spent the money and the time to get there. *Let's just do it,* I thought.

But approaching the interview table and spotting Sanson in front of me by a grey concrete wall, I simply lost my nerve. My hands grew clammy. No guard was in sight. Off to my left I spotted a huge inmate covered with tattoos lifting weights in the yard. I walked directly up to this herculean creature and said, "My name is Gayle Swedmark, what's yours?"

"Tank Ruiz" he mumbled.

"Would you like to be my assistant?" I asked. I think I trembled a little.

"Sure." He beamed at me.

"Your assignment, Mr. Ruiz, will be to handle these legal files and to keep order," I said.

"Yessum." He beamed again, gold tooth sparkling. We marched together back across the sandy yard to my metal interview table. "Mr. Sanson," I said, "this is my assistant, Mr. Ruiz." They stared at each other. They did not shake hands. I got my work done and drove back to Tampa to catch the flight home to Tallahassee.

Oh, yes, I sent a letter to the warden thanking him for the good job Mr. Tank Ruiz did in assisting me with the pretrial conference. I wonder if he ever figured it out. At least it is in the file for Inmate #72608, Mr. Tank Ruiz, Esquire.

The Johnson v. Boone Case

One of the most stressful and emotionally draining cases I had was the Johnson v. Boone case in Circuit Court in Leon County, Honorable Ted Steinmeyer presiding. A former top official of the Florida Department of Law Enforcement and his wife sued Leon County Sheriff Eddie Boone, his Undersheriff Larry Campbell, and Deputy Mike Troelstrup for falsely arresting them and charging abuse of her son. There was no claim that Boone was personally involved and he testified that no "order from the top" was given to arrest Danny and Lee Ellen Johnson. Campbell said that he did not direct Troelstrup, a school resource officer to whom Wallace had reported abuse, to make an arrest but that the son himself provided the necessary information, together with other evidence. On the witness stand the son, Wallace, gave anguished testimony about his stepfather slapping and berating him and said that his stepfather had a drinking problem. He thanked the cops for getting him out of a living hell. His sister, Tracy Eastman, backed up his testimony and told the jury that she, too, was estranged from her mother and stepfather. Whatever the facts of abuse or punishment, the law enforcement officers felt they had probable cause to arrest. It is clear to me now that some kind of family intervention was needed at a much earlier point, well before the arrest. It was painful to hear the hurts of a family. Plaintiffs' attorney said that the arrest was a big piece of garbage and that the acts complained about were punishment deserved within a parent's authority, not child abuse. Danny Johnson, the husband, lost his $70,000 job supervising 530 people. His wife claimed to have tried suicide by taking an overdose of pills prescribed for depression. An accountant for the plaintiff estimated that damages could reach $5.6 million.

The attorneys for the Johnsons tried every manner of intimidation and tactics. They accused me of kamikaze tactics and of "throwing caution to the wind" and told me that my clients would face financial ruin when the verdict came in. They tried to make me blink. They wanted us to settle. My co-counsel, John Jolly, represented Mike Troelstrup. Back at the office at night we talked about our situation.

"John, what do you think? Do we dare hold out? We will be in a mess if we lose," I said.

"Let's tee it up," he said. "I think the jury likes my client. You can keep damages down if they find against your people."

We called it a day. As we headed to the parking lot, we agreed that we should hold tight. We believed the law and facts were on our side. Of course, we could not know what a jury would do.

On February 6, 1994, the plaintiffs' attorneys hand-delivered a demand letter to me for $2.2 million in exchange for what they said they would give us: Complete releases and settlement agreements as to all of our clients. This was the day before we were to make our closing statements to the jury. My hands felt clammy. My throat was dry. I was also tired from the stress of the trial and the relentless television and radio coverage. Some predicted doom. Most were favorable to us. I tried not to watch or to read the publicity, but others would tell me about it.

The next night the jury went out. A preview of its thinking came in the five and a half hours of deliberations when the forewoman asked in writing: "Can we award just one dollar or does it have to be more?"

Judge Steinmeyer answered, "Reread the jury instructions."

We waited a little longer. The verdict was read. When the jury gave them a total of two dollars, I was finally able to exhale. The jury found that Boone was not liable. Troelstrup was not liable. Campbell was not liable in his personal capacity. They found that nobody in the sheriff's office acted recklessly or intentionally. At last the three-year ordeal was over.

More Normal Clients and Days

During my first year of practice, a kind looking little man came to my door and asked in a meek voice if I had the time to look at a contract. Of course I was thrilled to have a client of my own that the partners did not have to give to me. He taught at FSU and said he had never had a lawyer before. He was polite and mannerly, a thoughtful client. Before the day was over, I found out that he was Paul A.M. Dirac, Nobel Prize winner in physics. I was surprised to learn that his brother-in-law had also won a Nobel Prize in a different area. I asked him, "What do you people talk about at the dinner table at Thanksgiving?" It was rarified air for me, but I found him to be sweet and thoughtful through our relationship. He gave me a place setting of Minton china that he got on a trip to England where he was knighted by the queen. I am positive that his wife selected it. The image of Dr. Dirac in a china store buying a thank you gift is foreign to me. There is now a drive named for him in Tallahassee. He was Einstein's right hand man. Einstein was fond of saying, "Where is my Dirac?" I learned from Dirac that great people can be humble and nice.

A guy who wasn't so humble but was certainly nice was my next famous client. It was a minor dredge and fill issue concerning land in South Florida. The Supreme Court had agreed to hear the issue and they needed a Tallahassee lawyer familiar with an obscure statute. Me. He arrived with a battery of lawyers who came from Chicago and some from Miami. They had been litigating the matter for over fourteen years. I finished it up in four months and charged him $6,000. He was my friend until he died. He was John D. MacArthur, the man you hear credited with a foundation, along with his wife Catherine T. MacArthur. He was six times richer than Aristotle Onassis. At the time I represented him, he had approximately $3 billion and Aristotle was under $600 million. Mr. Mac, as we called him, told me he wanted split pea soup for his birthday. I got a birthday present from him also, a painting that had been in J.P. Morgan's library.

Mr. Mac was a character. He was once described as looking like a retired postman on social security. His clothes were never extravagant. His office was a corner table in the coffee shop at the Colonnades, one of his hotels in Palm Beach Gardens. He told me once that you can only wear one suit of clothes at a time and eat one meal at a time. The rest is excess. He hosted Daddy when Pop went to Palm Beach for a business meeting. He helped me when my mother died. He sent me a bolt of fabric with the MacArthur tartan from a mill he had. He said I had earned it. When I had a child, Mr. Mac took him for rides on the carousel in his bar at one of his hotels during the day when the bar was closed. Once, when he was ill, he asked me to smuggle bourbon into the hospital to him. He had a party exactly one year from the date of his death and invited us all to eat and drink and mingle in Palm Beach Gardens where he had spent so much time. On the film we reviewed there he commented: "I knew you all would be busy and wanted you to have plenty of notice for my funeral. Enjoy each other. Talk about me. Have fun. It is on the house." He was a memorable man.

The MacArthur Foundation sent me to Aurora, Illinois, for the grand opening of a theatre the foundation had saved and refurbished. Ed Asner, the actor, was the keynote speaker. He attended a reception for artists and musicians with me and, as he said, "People keep trying to make us a couple." He explained that I was an attorney from Tallahassee and not his companion, but he was sweet enough to say that he was honored. He was nice and friendly without pretention. The night after the ceremony he bought ice cream for all of the out-of-town guests. He said, "Meet me at the pool in an hour. It will be fun."

When I arrived outside to meet the group, Burl Ives was sitting on the diving board, playing his guitar. We had a lovely time, talking and visiting until midnight. Maureen O'Hara was sitting at a table by the pool, looking pretty and wearing a one-piece lilac swim suit with a white cotton lace cover up. She motioned for me to come over to her table and asked, "What was Mr. MacArthur really like? Was he a good guy or was he a son of a gun?"

I said, "He was one of a kind, Miss O'Hara. Did you know that Helen Hayes was his sister-in-law? She married playwright Charles MacArthur, who was his brother."

"Yes, I did know that. His nephew, their son, also had a part in *Hawaii Five-O*. There are some negative things written about Mr. Mac, but I have heard other people who liked him a lot."

"He had a quick mind and was a little impatient with laziness," I said. I went on to explain how he hated bureaucracy and he could use some pretty salty language when government wasted money and time. I also mentioned that he didn't like people to wait on him, and told how he always got out and opened the gate when I drove him out to our little country property in Tallahassee.

"He was also thoughtful, though, in little ways," I said. "He brought me a tiny glass dish from his old house in Chicago because it had a dog like mine etched in the center. And he had a killer sense of humor."

"I love a sense of humor and I can't stand laziness either," she said. "He sounds like somebody I would have liked."

"He would have liked you, too, Miss O'Hara. In fact, he probably did like your movies. I just bet he did. I know that he watched the John Wayne movies, so he probably saw that one about Ireland. I just know he would have loved you in it."

"I hope so," she said.

Thank goodness he came into my life in that unusual way for work on such an obscure statute that I happened to know something about.

Another client came to me in a strange way. It was about five o'clock on a football weekend in Tallahassee and most people were either leaving the office early or anxious to get away. The receptionist came to me and said there was a man who needed to see a lawyer.

"He is clean, but he doesn't look fancy," she said.

I reluctantly agreed. Somehow I thought it our job to be

available to the public, even those not prosperous or famous. As I went to greet him, I noticed an intelligent look and piercing blue eyes. He was business-like. He didn't waste any time telling me that he wanted to purchase a piece of property. It turned out to be Water Oak Plantation in Tallahassee. He was a fine man and became a wonderful client.

Tallahassee and Thomasville have quite a few plantations and, as a result, attract money and famous families. Polly Carnegie came to me from her home on a large tract of land out in Lamont near Perry. She walked in one morning and told me that she was a liberal who wanted to give women a chance whenever she could. I told her that I would not take her case unless I thought it was within my field of knowledge. It was. We liked each other right away. When she found out that I was from Fernandina, we had happy chatter about Cumberland Island. The Carnegies had been ensconced there since right after the time of the Nathaniel Green land grant. They attended the church of my childhood when they took water transportation on the short ride over to Fernandina.

Polly had been married to Carter Beggs Carnegie, who died in 1957. He was the son of Thomas Morrison Carnegie. She had one son named Henry, who had been adopted by Carter as an adult, in 1956. When Polly and Carter lived in Lamont, Henry was jokingly called Sir Henry of Lamont by his mother, but as an adult he moved to Paris and we called him Henri of Paris. His daughter Suzanne was a sweet child whose mother, according to Polly, had left Henry for a ski instructor. Polly made me trustee for Suzanne for a time. Lance, my son, adored them both and when Suzanne was in America she spent a lot of time with us. Polly wanted Henry and me to make a match but there was no interest there on either side. He was attractive and did seem like a very fine intelligent gentleman. He once admired a painting that I had been given by John D. MacArthur for my thirtieth birthday. I suppose he had excellent taste.

In the case of *Carnegie et al. v. First National Bank of Brunswick, Trustee, et al. (129 SE2d 780 (1963),* the Georgia Superior Court in Camden County held that Henry was entitled to a share of the Cumberland Island, Georgia, property under the will of his great-grandmother, even though he was adopted. That seemed to me to be an obvious decision. Polly always had a fondness for the Cumberland Island area. It is the place where John F. Kennedy, Jr. married Caroline Bessette.

Once I was taking Polly to Fernandina for a visit to Cumberland Island when we were struck in the rear by an eighteen wheeler on I-95 north of Jacksonville. When we came to a halt across the median in the far on-coming lane of traffic, our car was pretty mangled. The trunk lid was protruding into the back seat of the car. I was happy to hear a little voice from the floor of the passenger side front seat say, "Carter gave me those earrings!" I knew that she was able to talk and to think. It was a relief. I met a lifelong friend that night, Trooper Dave Barclay, who pulled us out of the car with the Jaws of Life and got us checked out at the local hospital. He says Polly and I were quite a sight. Polly was admitted for injury to her arm. I went on out to the Amelia Island Plantation and had a deviled crab and a sip of a beer. I introduced Dave to a friend of mine and they saw each other for some time. He has two beautiful daughters of whom he is extremely proud. His son-in-law Zach Johnson won the Masters Golf Tournament in Augusta in 2007. Once Dave was on the venire panel for a jury I was selecting in Fernandina. When he said that he knew me and had met me in a wreck, he was about to be excused. As he was walking down from the jury box, I heard him say, in an attempt to help me out, "She was one of the bravest I ever saw." We had a good laugh about that when I saw him later. I wasn't especially brave but I was cool headed. I was just happy to see that my dear friend Polly was not seriously injured. She was a person I thoroughly enjoyed being with. She was a fine lady.

Some people with whom I came in contact were not so fine. I have wondered how people with similar starts in life can be so different. I have wondered how people can be mean in a world full of wonder and beauty. Is it nature or nurture? Environment or heredity? A killer who savaged our town made us all wonder about that.

Ted Bundy

The name Bundy brings chills to me to this day. I have no opinion on the subject of how evil transmits or whether it is caused by nature or nurture, environment or genes. I do believe that some people are evil. Ted Bundy was one of those.

Here is how I first met him. Our law firm represented sheriffs around the state, and specifically I represented the Leon County Sheriff for forty years. Prisoners are allowed to sue the sheriff over conditions of confinement since his office operates the jail in most counties. He may be sued regarding food quality, medical care, and exercise availability. Prisoners can file suit with or without an attorney. In some, though not all, cases the suit gives them a chance to get out of jail to go to court, to be on TV or to have an opportunity to escape. Many suits are frivolous. Ted sued the Sheriff of Leon County, claiming that the lighting in his cell was not adequate to allow him to help his attorney prepare for his murder trials. At our weekly partner's conference the boys reasoned that I wasn't Bundy's type. They decided that I would be safe with him and should be the one to defend this case and be Ted's opponent. "After all," they reasoned, "he likes young girls with dark hair parted in the middle and you aren't—well, young." Soon the file was in my office and I was making an appointment with the classification officer to meet with him out at Appleyard Drive at the jail. The court required me to meet with him to work out certain stipulations of the case.

Since Bundy was a high security risk and had escaped twice from two different institutions, he wasn't allowed to come to the conference room. I went up to his cell, going through the usual metal doors that banged behind me. For privacy reasons, I couldn't take the correctional officers in with me, though they could stand discreetly within sight so I could yell and motion if any problem occurred.

To say that I felt evil emanating from that cell would be an understatement. I already knew what he had done to so many young women and had seen crime scene photographs from the Chi Omega house in Tallahassee. It wasn't a premonition. It was a fact. I was afraid. Logically, there was no cause to fear. Emotionally, I could imagine demons, yes. My throat was a little dry. Bundy was studiously and sarcastically polite. He had a sneer and a wry smirk the whole time, obviously hoping to make me feel uncomfortable. I bluffed, didn't blink, and sat right next to him on his bunk. He took the papers I handed him to read with a great ceremony. His feet in the shower shoes issued to inmates were ugly and gnarled. They were grotesque. I thought of a cartoon drawing of evil. He was not handsome as he was portrayed in the media, probably because the prison pallor gave him a grey cast. His features were hawk-like because he had lost weight, probably hoping to escape through any small space he later found.

His last words to me were, "I will be in touch."

"I will be keeping up with you," I said.

GAYLE SWEDMARK HUGHES

"Nice meeting you, Mrs. Swedmark."

I said, in the sweetest voice I could muster, "I hope your murder trials turn out the way they should."

Ophelia Givens Dickey

The pace of the law practice was picking up. I had become president of the Big Bend Medical Foundation and was on the Chamber of Commerce Board of Directors. Soon I was elected president of Tallahassee Community College Foundation. I noticed that as the weeks grew busier and the hours more demanding I needed help managing a household and the chores. Ossie Lee Sutton, from Havana, helped me until she decided to marry a preacher man and move to Augusta. I asked her to find somebody nice to help me at least once a week. What resulted was an absolute Gift from God just as though He had wrapped her up and put a big bow on her with a note that read, "This woman will make your life better in every way."

Ophelia Dickey, a mahogany woman of great dignity, showed up dressed in good taste, and she was soft-spoken. I met her at the door and said, "It is such a beautiful day, do you want to walk and talk?"

"Yes ma'am."

"Ophelia, what do you like to do best?"

"I like tending to little children. If I could have had the money, I would surely have built a place for them that don't have a home. Yes ma'am I would have."

"You don't have to say that, you know."

"I don't have to say what?"

"Yes ma'am," I said.

114

"Yes ma'am," she said. "I know."

"What kind of people don't you like, Ophelia?"

"I don't know. I don't really say how anybody should do. I try to live right. By the Bible. Other people you know . . . I can't say what they do. It takes all kinds to make it. People are all the same to me. It doesn't matter what color. How much money. All the same to me."

"How do you feel about lying?" I asked.

She scrunched up her face and made a disgusted look. She said nothing for a long while. We walked.

"Is there anything about housework that you don't care much for?"

"Well," she said, "I don't like ironing all that much. But I will do it, if the Lord says so."

We walked back up the lane.

"O.K. Ophelia. If you will stand by me and help me and be faithful to me, I will get us somebody good to iron for both of us. I don't have any babies for you to keep, but someday I hope to. I will be good to you as I know how. Tell me your worries and come to me with your troubles and we will figure it all out together. Fair enough?"

"Well . . . it's all right, I reckon," she said.

In the forty-six years that we were together, Ophelia became my mother, sister, friend, chaplain and psychologist. We laughed together, we cried together. When my son came along seven years after she came to work with me, she seemed happy to have a little person to raise and to keep her company again. She had raised thirteen of her own children and was my reference book on child rearing. She helped me select my husband about whom she said, "This is the one. He IS the one." When my father was elderly, he came out to the house to sit and talk with her by his side. She kept him company while we were at work. Without her by my side, I could never have had the successful career that I did.

On her eightieth birthday, my husband went out to her church and took a picture of her coming out the door. She had on an azalea colored hat and matching dress and looked like a princess.

She retired in August of 2008. I went out to her house and sat on her porch and we read the Bible together. We both had a serious disease by then. I gave her eulogy in January of 2009. I said, "Ophelia is like that tree that is planted by the water. She cannot be moved. When I was down, she brought me up and when I was too far up, she brought me down. I miss you, Ophelia."

Welcome to the World, Lance Chandler

On a Friday afternoon in the winter, our office seemed particularly quiet. A woman sitting in the client chair was taking the long way around to tell me her story. Daddy would have said that if you asked her what time it was she would explain how to make a watch. I was getting increasingly impatient because the contractions as I timed them were close to seven minutes apart.

"Excuse me," I said. "I am in labor and I need to gather some things up to take to the hospital." As it turned out, I had plenty of time. Sunday night on January 30, 1972, about 5:30 p.m.—suppertime in the South—Lance Chandler Swedmark was born by Caesarian section. He was a lucky 7 pounds, 11 ounces. As I combed my hair to meet him and put on a nice blue and white checkered gown, I thought how I would be able to care for him and teach him life's lessons. I prayed that he would have a decent and happy life. It had never been my plan to be an attorney with no children. The idea of motherhood had always been important to me. I was about to find out how the balancing act could be accomplished. It seems, in looking back, that with the help of God and Ophelia, I was able to provide well for his physical and emotional needs. He has turned out to be a great guy, a fine man, who is loved by many people and who cares deeply for other folks. I will not take the credit for that. At least not all of the credit.

TWO THOUSAND DAFFODILS

At first he came along to my office in a little basket and I put it under my desk. Later he slept while I worked on Saturday mornings. He played on the floor as he grew older and then he began to feel at home there and read in the library. Sometimes he visited with the other attorneys. He especially enjoyed Governor Caldwell, a tall man, who played with him.

If Bundy was the most sinister person I met in practice—and he probably was—the most remarkable, finest example of public service and professionalism to come across my path was Millard Filmore Caldwell.

Governor Caldwell

Remembered as civil defense administrator under President Harry S. Truman, Governor Caldwell is the man who helped me get my first job with Judge Sturgis. When he retired from the Supreme Court of Florida as chief justice, he came to the firm and became my law partner. It strikes me often that my life involved being in the right place at the right time. Governor Caldwell, or "Skipper" as we called him, loved his wife "Miss Mary" and his daughters, bourbon, playing gin rummy, dogs, and reading. He was impatient with tardiness.

Once, when the entire cabinet was late to a regularly scheduled meeting, he adjourned and told the press gathered there, "Gentlemen, we simply do not do business that way." Another time, when he was ready to go back to the mansion and his Highway Patrol assigned driver was missing, he simply got in and drove himself home. He was strong willed. When *Collier* magazine accused him of making a racist statement, he sued them, won, and donated the money to Florida A&M University.

When I was pregnant with son Lance Chandler, I received a visit from Governor Caldwell in my office very early one morning. He stretched his long well-tailored legs across the corner of my desk and said, "This is the first and last time I will talk to you about child rearing. First, you cannot impart a damn thing to the youth. Secondly, they have a right to make their own mistakes."

When son Lance was a toddler, I would take him to the office on Saturday morning and he usually sat on the floor drawing, coloring, and pretending to read law books. One morning when I looked up, I missed him and found him in Judge Caldwell's office where he was gently tugging on the Judge's pants leg. Caldwell was saying into the phone, "I have to go now, Ellis. There is a client here." Then he hung up on Governor Ellis Arnall of Georgia and lifted Lance up to go and drink out of the water fountain. It was a Saturday ceremony for them. Caldwell had always enjoyed his good conversations with Governor Arnall although they were political opposites. Judge Caldwell loved a good debate, but he insisted that it be civilized and cordial.

Judge Caldwell appreciated brevity. Once I sent him a detailed memorandum analyzing a situation with respect to one of his clients. His response was succinct: "Sue." How fortunate I was to try my skills among such stalwart political and legal figures. For the most part I was healthy and happy. Once in a while I had a detour.

Was It a Near-Death Experience?

One afternoon I was attending a ball game when I had a piercing pain. It made me dizzy and when I got in the car I dialed my doctor, Jesse Judelle. He told me to meet him at the emergency room at Tallahassee Memorial Hospital. Caring and brilliant, Judelle sized it up correctly and got a surgeon, Eliott Sieloff, involved with us. That night I was diagnosed as being critically septic with peritonitis from ruptured internal undiscovered abdominal abscesses. Two weeks later I was well enough to have a colon resection removing five feet of my intestines. The resection, thankfully, was done in one stage without the humiliation of external parts. It was not cancer. It was, however, excruciatingly painful. A Pakistani nurse sat with me during the night. My friend Mason came to see me and sat by my bed. I remember trying to call out to her and not being able to. Ann brought flowers from her lovely garden and I held one in my palm as I went to sleep. It was a time of strange thoughts and sensations. Here is what I recall about the images two weeks prior to surgery when they were trying to get the infection and fever under control enough to operate. Quite honestly I am not absolutely certain what part the morphine drip in my arm played in the experience. Clearly it did not cause all, or nearly all, of this.

I was suspended between two opposite planes of reality, liberated from gravity. Free and soaring, I was in a kind of

121

nirvana until I was pulled back by a piercing pain and the knowledge that I was actually still alive.

Compassionate faces came by the screen of my vision murmuring consoling and reassuring things. These were faces familiar to me from my present world. Still, I wanted to leave the pain. Back I slipped to the comfort of surrendering.

A creative and spiritual tide connected me, then, to the universal spirit of loveliness and purity and holiness. All of the energy on the planet was mine. The energy seemed to stream through all of my senses. I was, at that moment, perfect, whole, unified and beautiful. For that moment I was at one with all that is.

This experience is one reason I am no longer afraid of death. During that dreamlike phase I have described I felt people lifting me up in prayer. I felt that strength. I saw the faces of Anna, Aunt Ruth, Ophelia and then of my son and husband. My husband called me back. When I awakened, he was holding my hand. Soon I was back on the job and looking forward to a new adventure.

The Handcuff Case

Representing Sheriff Jake Miller of Brevard County, Florida, I had a case where a young man claimed to have been injured by the tight handcuffs that he alleged were improperly placed upon him by arresting officers. He testified upon deposition that he could not lift his arm above his waist and that he was severely limited in caring for himself and enjoying life as a result of our deputy's negligence. He was a sad witness. I had no idea as to the merits of the case medically, so I employed both a doctor to examine him and an investigator to observe him. Neither came up with anything definite although my doctor personally believed the plaintiff was faking it. He couldn't prove it. The opposing attorney was what we commonly call a bottom feeder and demanded an exorbitant amount of money. Usually I try to be cordial and professional with all opponents but this one tried my patience.

About a month before trial, the sheriff's secretary called me in Tallahassee and said, "Mrs. Swedmark, I don't know if it matters or not but I think I saw Mr. Downy playing volleyball on TV."

My heart began to pound and my face got warm. "Do you know anyone else who might have seen him?" I tried not to sound too excited. She thought there may be a tape of the game. It was part of the Semi-Pro Beach Volleyball program in Cocoa Beach. She found a copy of the tape and called me back.

I said, "Let the sheriff know that we won't be settling this one." The following week I happily played the tape for opposing counsel and he advised his client that the only sensible course was to dismiss the case. The plaintiff strangely enough still wanted to go to trial. It was easy and fun. The easiest I ever had. It was much shorter than the normal case. I read from the transcript of the deposition about his claimed injuries and limitations. Then I played the tape of the volleyball game, the plaintiff jumping, yelling and kicking sand and all. The jury stayed out seventeen minutes.

A Pistol for a Gift

Some of the sheriffs took a paternalistic attitude towards me when I was a little younger. I encouraged it by asking their advice. One old-timey sheriff from Central Florida was taking me to the airport in Tampa and handed me a small pistol, called a lemon squeezer with hollow point bullets. A hollow point bullet is an expanding bullet that has a pit in its tip, generally intended to expand upon entering a target and to disrupt more as it travels through the target. It is made to cause destruction. A lemon squeezer is a little snub nose revolver, Model 40 sold by Smith and Wesson. The pistol was very sensitive to touch. The name comes from a safety feature in the pistol grip that prevents firing unless the pistol is gripped firmly and the trigger is pulled, so that the safety release is manually activated. It is used widely for law enforcement, and the hammerless concept makes it easy to shoot simply by squeezing hard. In my case it was too easy.

The sheriff said, "Here, take this for your protection. It doesn't have a serial number on it, and it's small enough for you. Do you know how to use a firearm?"

I said, "Of course I do. All of my life." I grabbed hard at the pistol at the same time that he hit a bump in the road. I shot through his police radio, his regular radio and his air conditioning. The noise was fierce. I was mortified. I scratched the powder burns on my leg through my stockings. We stopped at a warehouse on the truck route so I could

125

wash my legs with a hose. My apologies streamed out and he laughed.

He said, "The big problem is how to get the car fixed. Guess I will have to tell them I was chasing a fleeing felon and sitting low in my seat." He was nice about it. I think he was later indicted for something and maybe went to prison, but he was nice to me that day. One day at the office I received an envelope with a spent shell. I made a plexiglass paperweight to remind me of what a fool we can be when we least expect it.

GAYLE SWEDMARK HUGHES

Business Trip to Lisbon, Portugal

Working with distinguished lawyers and people active in the bar associations brought me some enviable opportunities. It was on one of those ordinary workdays, full of dreary chores, when my senior partner Jack Madigan buzzed me and asked me if I wanted to go to Lisbon, Portugal, for a legal seminar, to appear on a panel representing women lawyers in America. For a single parent on the way out of the door to the dry cleaners and the shoe repair shop, this sounded pretty exotic and wonderful. After finding out the date and details, I called Daddy and said, "Can you go to Portugal with me?" He agreed. It turned out to be one of our most memorable times together. We soon flew to New York City and then in to Lisbon, called Lisboa by the locals.

Portugal charmed me probably more than any place ever, mostly due to the gentleness and kindness of its people. There, where the annual income was about $2,000 per person, the jacket was nicely patched and well cleaned and pressed. The modest little offering in the home of bread was often accompanied by a butter pat in the shape of a flower, and the caldo verde, or green soup, was served in a nice old pottery bowl. In Portugal, unlike Spain, the bull is not killed, or even stabbed. He is sort of poked a little with a dull stick and maneuvered about to music. Even the dreaded political upheavals in the 1980s involved primarily the bombing of empty buildings. FADO clubs, unlike our bars, have a quiet shushing sound to the conversation, more like the ocean than a jukebox or the loud jabber you would hear in our clubs.

Daddy, my law partner Jack, his wife Marylou and I went on the train over to Estoril, where the World War II spies hung out and the casinos were full of European names. Daddy liked the jingle of the one-armed bandits, Jack and his wife preferred the shows, and I played poker with a couple of German decorators.

I saw the white peacocks in the gardens at the Ritz in Lisbon and, in one of those serendipitous moments that has marked my life, I ran into a former Iowa Law School classmate in the revolving door leaving the Ritz.

He said, "Gayle?"

I said, "Steve?" and then it was a question of how much time I had left before going to the airport. Steve, who worked for a petroleum company that had an office there, insisted on touring the Alfama and Castille St. George and other areas until time for me to check out and meet our group at the airport. My philosophy was I could always sleep on the plane.

The most meaningful time of that trip, however, was meeting a widow, dressed all in black, and lugging manure for her garden on her donkey up the hills. She spoke a tiny bit of English and we were able to say a few words in Portuguese together. Her dignity and pride were so obvious when, she who had nothing, invited me in to soup. She made sure that we said grace. I liked her so much. Maria Batista Blanco was typical of the proud people of Portugal.

Without the contacts I made through the law firm, I would never have had many of the opportunities, experiences, and travel the other partners encouraged me to do.

It was not all glamorous, however. Some assignments were light years from the capitals of Europe and I did a good bit of driving up and down Interstate 10 and stopping at truck stops for coffee. Goodness knows I put in more than my share of hours in sparsely settled areas of rural north Florida.

Florida State Prison at Raiford

The prison is on parched ground out in the piney woods in a remote area near Starke. It is infamous for the macabre sight of crowds shown on television with coolers and lawn chairs attending executions. The facility is actually much more than that. It has libraries, computer classrooms, medical units, sports medicine and even two small courtrooms way back in the depths of the prison. A long walk leads from the visitors' parking area to the entrance to the administration building. From there, another walk takes you past the tower and the barbed wire security checkpoints. In all of those areas trustees work on the scant shrubbery and raking the grounds.

Sometimes at Raiford I was almost fearful for my life. Once I was taking a deposition of James Knight, serial killer, when the power went off. Terrified, with James across the table from me, I said in my best bossy voice, "James, keep talking, just keep talking. I mean it. I want to know where you are every minute or you will be in serious trouble." He complied. My hands were clammy for the entire six minutes until the generator was brought on line. It seemed like six hours.

Most vivid to me is a small non-jury trial that I had one November afternoon deep inside the prison. Judge Harvey Schlessinger was on the bench in a courtroom less than fourteen feet wide and about that length. The walls were cheap plywood and the seats were varnished church-style benches without pads. The legal issue was whether or not it was constitutionally permissible to shackle certain categories of inmates. I stood facing the judge, arguing the case law that permitted such restraints for extremely dangerous inmates during transport. My client, the very large and very sweet teddy bear of a guy, Tommy Seagraves, major with Nassau County Sheriff's Office, was by my side. As I spoke, the Judge looked behind me and his face seemed transfixed on the scene. His expression was contorted by shock. I whirled around to see what Judge Schlessinger was looking at. A prisoner in an orange jumpsuit was in the process of stabbing another prisoner to death.

The event we were witnessing had nothing to do with my own case, but the area had to be roped off and secured as a crime scene. I had immediately and instinctively tucked myself into and under the substantial side of Major Seagraves and put my face downward into the bend of his shirt sleeve. I didn't even make an attempt to be brave. Judge Schlessinger said, "We are now in recess. Maybe we all need a break. We will continue this case until next Thursday at 1 p.m. Have a safe drive back home, Gayle." I think he might have been a little shaken too although he never showed any sign of it.

Not all cases were dramatic. Some were routine. They were all different. So that I might give a more detailed first person account of the feel of a normal trial, if there is such a thing, I have pulled the next section from my own diary written contemporaneously with a federal trial of the sort I was doing a lot of. Except for an interesting finale, it is pretty much the way a young lawyer might expect the scenario to play out in a jury trial.

The Adam Parsons Verdict

It was a crisp cold day in north Florida. I had cooked Texas cornbread before work in the morning and left a slow cooker of chili plugged in to stew all day. Oak logs were stacked neatly in the fireplace to start later. Hopefully there could be a victory celebration. If not, a comfortable homecoming would be a nice consolation after the week in trial. My soft wool suit and blouse felt just right for the day.

As I entered the federal courthouse, I looked appreciatively at the murals representing the signing of the Magna Charta and other significant moments in man's struggle for justice. A graphic depicted the terrible turmoil in Selma, Alabama, when the civil rights movement was awakening. This building was timeless with its massive halls, marble floors and carved jury rails. I waved at the courthouse staff, acknowledging their warm greetings, and glanced at my cocky opponent walking up the steps. *I have blouses older than he is,* I thought. Still, his closing argument had been excellent. He was capable.

Adam Parsons, my client, was sitting on the mahogany bench just past the security screening area, waiting. He looked like the former Eagle Scout that he was, six feet solidly built, with blue eyes and sandy hair.

"How do you think we did?" he said. "Did you see the way number three juror looked at you during closing?"

"Three" had been a square-shouldered lady with blue

black hair we called "Elvira" among ourselves. During jury selection she seemed to have a strong personality and the smart money was on her for foreman. "Watch her during the judge's instructions," I suggested. We entered the courtroom together, passing in to counsel table through a low wooden swinging gate nudged open by Adam's left knee.

"All rise," the Marshall called out and Judge William Sterling, United States District Judge for the Northern District of Florida, entered. His kind eyes twinkled, crow's feet framing his humor. "Counsel, I do apologize for being five minutes late, but my wife parked behind my truck and I had to wake her to find the keys to her car. Not a happy occasion." Everyone chuckled. "Before I call the jury in for instructions, I wanted to see whether any of you lawyers have objections or additions to the final version of the written charges you have been furnished this morning."

The charge conference in chambers had lasted two hours on Thursday night and there were no further comments to be put on the record by counsel. Purdue, for the plaintiff, half rose and said, "None, Judge."

I stood. "No further requests your honor."

"Very well, then. Let's bring in the jury."

"I will now instruct you on the law to be applied to the facts of this case," Judge Sterling began.

Adam appeared to retreat to his own thoughts. He may have been reflecting on the days before when he had to listen to witnesses second guessing his actions as a Madison County deputy. His wedding was only three weeks away. He had an unblemished record and was not known as a rogue cop. Yet, he had only a few seconds to react to a situation where a wife and child were threatened with immediate death. From our earlier talks, I knew he wondered if he could have done anything different, if he could have taken Lloyd Freeman down without that shot.

The facts were this: A young woman over in Madison, Florida, had called the sheriff because her husband had threatened, once again, to kill her and their young son. Adam had approached the house, called for backup, and in the struggle with the armed man eventually had shot Lloyd. The wife sued Sheriff Peavy, who was now dismissed from the case, and also Adam, for the harm they did to her husband. She asked damages of $42 million. It was an obvious shakedown. My fear was, though, that the sympathy for the widow would send this jury off track. Or that one anti-law enforcement person could hang the jury. The widow had cried on the stand and told a version that she possibly now believed and that featured Adam as the villain.

The trial had been full of witness testimony that the husband had mercilessly beaten his wife Janet on numerous occasions, sending her to the hospital several times.

Nurse Cindy Wallace, a pert brunette, testified, "We saw Ms. Freeman on a regular basis for 'falling down' bruises and abrasions. Once I gave her the number for the Madison County Crisis Center."

Dr. Mark Patterson, a graying and distinguished man, described his treatment of Janet for broken bones. "Mr. Freeman even threatened me once in E.R. and accused me of interfering with his marriage. I assured him that I would have him physically removed from the hospital if he ever challenged me again. Deputy Parsons came to the door to see if he should be of assistance that night. It was clear to both of us that the man had a propensity for violence. He tested positive for cocai—" he started to say.

"Objection!" shouted Purdue.

"Sustained," Judge Sterling said. There could be no evidence presented in this case of Freeman's prior drug use on the ground that it was irrelevant and would prejudice the jury.

During the third day of trial, Agent Curt Simmons, Florida Department of Law Enforcement, took the stand. The jury loved his ease and soft spoken manner. He had a sort of bookish sex appeal. He was lanky and tall and wore rimless glasses. Simmons testified that the angle of the bullet upon entry and the position of the body supported the testimony of Adam Parsons. Standing near the jury box, he gave a PowerPoint presentation stating, "These photographs indicate blood spatter consistent with the deceased having been standing above the deputy at the time of the shot. Mr. Freeman's pistol was also discharged twice prior to his death. This bullet fragment on the lower step is from Mr. Freeman's own weapon and was aimed in the direction of the deputy."

Marguerita Arruzo, Medical Examiner from Jacksonville, made staccato sounds with her heels on the marble floors as she came to the stand. A tiny mighty mouse with a Spanish accent, she was almost too irreverent when speaking of the deceased. She confirmed the trajectory of the bullet in the body and that the fatal shot was practically inevitable in the struggle. As Dr. Arruzo testified, I had seen two of my former partners slip into the back row of the courtroom. It was a show of solidarity, providing a kind of moral support. My level of sharpness was turned up and it helped energize me for the final laps of the case. Bill Martin winked at me and Jack Colson smiled approvingly later as I returned to my seat at counsel table after closing argument.

Adam looked back up now as Judge Sterling concluded his instructions to the jury and sent them out for deliberations. "Ms. Swedmark," the judge said, "you and your folks may use the grand jury room and you, Mr. Purdue, and your clients are to be situated in the conference room on the opposite end of this floor. You all will discover that the Uptown Café is pretty decent and it makes deliveries if you wish. Good day for now."

As we found comfortable seating around a conference table in the grand jury room, Adam held out the chair for me. "Miss Gayle," he said, "No matter what happens, I just want you to know that . . ."

"I know. I know." I sighed, slipping my right foot out of the soft camel Tommy Hilman pump. I enjoyed the rich-as-sin leather smell as I used my toe to rub the top of my left foot. I felt comfortable with this young man and he with me.

We waited. Adam checked the oak schoolhouse clock overhead. 10:30 a.m. The sheriff peaked in the door. "Are they back yet?" he joked.

"No."

He came silently in, edging his way behind the chairs

around the table. He patted Adam's shoulder and made a massaging gesture. Dressed in civilian clothes, like most Florida sheriffs, Joe Peavy looked more like a banker. Recently married to his second wife, Suzanne, he was becoming more stylish. He was respected and loyal to his troops. He was also known to be harsh on anyone caught using excessive force. Adam was obviously a favorite of the boss.

I stretched my arms out behind my back. The large hand moved to nine on the clock. 10:45. "I'm going for coffee. Anybody want anything?"

"Nope. Thanks," Adam said.

"Nothing for me," the sheriff echoed.

Downstairs I caught the canteen at a slow time. "I'll have a double latte with soy please, George," I joked, putting a one dollar bill on the glass case.

He touched my hand lightly and also the bill as he said, "Morning, pretty lady. When we gonna run off?"

"My perfect man," I replied. "Blind and employed."

He laughed as he poured bitter coffee from the bottom of a Mr. Coffee Pyrex carafe. Our private joke on the pretentiousness of Starbucks was lost on the folks in line behind me. They were hypnotized at the sight of a blind man pouring steaming liquid.

As I edged my way out and past the line forming in the canteen, I spotted the entire Freeman clan coming in. Avoiding eye contact, I felt some surge of sympathy for the family. Even though they were pretty trashy people, known for poaching and setting fires, I recognized that they had lost a family member. Tiny bristles rose on the back of my neck as I felt them glaring at me. I would be professional. Take the high road. No reason to antagonize them.

I stopped by the industrial style women's room. It had black and white hexagon tile floors. The light was unflatteringly harsh as I dabbed on pale peach lip gloss. I ran a quick brush through my hair. *Let's hope the jury comes back soon,* I thought. *Long times only mean trouble for us.*

Two hours later Adam drummed two fingers on his pants leg. I turned over a clean legal pad and wrote on the back: "Publix-shallots; Don's Shoe Shop-pick up dress sandals; Heritage Oaks-visit Mr. Quinley."

Focused on planning my Saturday morning chores, I flinched when the door cracked and my secretary Moira came in. "Bearing gifts," she called out, piling phone messages, a *New York Times*, and star mints on the conference table. "Hey, Adam, how about those Yankees?"

"No pitching," he said.

The sheriff got up and gave Moira a hug. "Lunchtime," he said. Punching numbers on his cell phone he asked the clerk at the Uptown Café for three chicken salads and a fruit plate delivered.

He looked questioningly at me for my order and then passed me the phone.

"Real turkey. Not that pressed stuff. Whole wheat pita please, mayo with some curry in it, and your mama's apricot preserves on the bread with watercress and walnuts. Thank you much, Lisa. Wish us luck. Sure. Hang on. Adam, she wants to talk to you."

She was Adam's cousin by marriage. Soon he laughed for the first time that day. Lisa had told him to remember to check his fly zipper and to call his Mom as soon as he heard the verdict. We had all agreed that having his family at the trial would have been obvious pandering to the jury and difficult on them as well.

At four-thirty Moira went back to the office.

"We have a verdict! We have a verdict!" called out the courtroom deputy Marvin Waits from out in the hall.

A light had come on over the bench to signal that the jury had reached a verdict. The equivalent of Vatican smoke, this is an almost universal courtroom signal. Sheriff Peavy went to look and to confirm that it was showing green. "A warm rush just moved up from my chest to my neck. If I ever lost the thrill of this moment in a trial, it would be time to quit this job. I slid on my shoes. Adam buttoned up his jacket. We scrambled together back into the courtroom.

"All rise." Judge Sterling came in, robe flapping in his wake. He sat and rapped his gavel. He cleared his throat and straightened the papers in front of him as he said, "Bring the jury in."

Elvira came in first, shoulders back, chin up. Confident, she looked at neither counsel. She had a paper in her hand. Yep. She was foreman.

"Ladies and gentlemen, have you reached a verdict?" Judge Sterling asked.

"We have your honor," answered Elvira.

Adam exhaled quietly.

The courtroom deputy received the paper and passed it

quickly to the judge to read aloud. "We, the jury, find in favor of the defendant Adam Parsons and therefore assess damages at zero."

I smiled a very discreet smile at Adam. He slumped towards me, leaning his head on my shoulder in joy and relief.

Crack! I heard someone scream and thought it was shots fired. A woman vaulted up on the first row seats. Joe Peavy leapt after her in hot pursuit. People began to dive under the benches. I soon realized the sound I'd heard was only wood cracking from the weight of the Claudine Freeman. The largest sister, the redhead, sailed on the swinging gate to counsel table. Janet was close behind her.

Adam jumped to block her way. *Time to run or dive under something,* I thought. I glanced back. A woman with rage on her face. Hell in her eyes. Right there upon me. Claudine lunged forward and reached out for me. She missed. I spun around, hitting the table. Janet stuck something sharp in my side. I bolted. A split second later blood spurted.

The marshals scrambled. Waits was on one side of me. Strong as a bull. A former Gator linebacker. The sheriff subdued Janet. Marshall Bobby Montgomery was on my other side. His broad hand was in the small of my back, pushing me out. A tide of fear and nausea washed over me. My ears pounded with thumping pressure.

Judge Sterling shouted from his chambers doorway, "Get her the hell out of here!"

As Marvin reached the small elevator behind the bench

ahead of the rest of them, he jammed the button with his finger. He shoved me in as the door slid open. Bobby and the other marshal were close to me as they tumbled in. Quickly we reached the basement. "So this is where this elevator goes," I said. "I saw something silver when she headed towards me. Was it really a knife?"

"No, a metal nail file. Should never have gotten past security." Bobby grumbled. He pushed me into the rear seat of a dark government sedan as he spoke. "You all right?" he said, pulling my blouse loose at the waist and dabbing my skin with a soft medicinal scented cloth.

"Yes, sir. I'm good. Most of the blood came from that arm scratch."

"I don't think they like you," Marvin drawled as he started the engine. As the broad garage doors opened upward the car took off westward and made a quick right on Duval Street. It is then that the younger Marshall took out his handheld and called the law office.

"We have had an incident and are en route to deliver Ms. Swedmark to her home," he told one of my partners. "No, you should not go to her house at this time. She is safe and will speak with you later. Thank you. Good day."

I gave directions and soon the shaded entry to my driveway on Oxbottom Road was visible. Gretel and Nash, my two large outdoor dogs, escorted the black sedan along the driveway, smiling broad dog smiles. I gave a side glance at the fall colors and the wind whipping the upper limbs of the dogwoods. I eased out of the rear seat. "You gentlemen care for a bowl of chili?"

GAYLE SWEDMARK HUGHES

The next week when thank you calls had been made and commendations written, there was a large white envelope in my mailbox. An invitation to Adam's wedding.

Oxbottom Road

Some of the older African Americans told me that Oxbottom Road gets its name because the ox carts used to get stuck down in the "bottom" coming off the hill at the turn. The ten acres I live on is between Rose Hill Plantation and Water Oak Plantation on the highest spot on the road. They said that the oxen would get stuck between the two plantations during our tropical rainy season.

In 1950 Sue Boynton, a pioneer family lady, and her late husband, W.J. Boynton, Jr., purchased a large tract of land now known as Oxbottom area. She told me that when oxen plowed the fields, a favorite place to find a runaway ox was the huge bottom lying between what is now Ox Bow and Evening Star roads. This bottom was full of maiden cane, a nutritious native plant, which oxen loved. Today it is a thriving residential area. Retired Lt. Colonel Albert Griffin purchased several hundred acres from the Boyntons for himself and his twin sister. When he sold me the property that has been our home for years, it was quite rural. The road was not completely paved. I boarded horses down the road at the old Boynton Homestead Stables for $60 each per month. I reasoned that a land payment might be a good investment instead of the boarding fees.

One fall Saturday afternoon I was riding my mare, La Lindata, through oak-dotted hills and by small bass ponds when I came upon a gentleman who greeted me kindly. He was Colonel Griffin, the owner of the land, but he welcomed me to ride on it. He had about a thousand acres at that time, the best I can figure. I liked him immediately. We talked a long while. I offered him iced tea from my saddlebag and said, "Do you want to sell this piece on the hill?"

He said, "My wife Helga would kill me. She wants to build a house here."

I said, "If you ever change your mind, could you at least give me a chance?" I handed him a slip of paper with my phone number on it. Some three years later he called. It has been my home for over forty-one years and the site of many picnics, receptions, teenagers ball games and family celebrations.

A row of dogwood trees that came from a nearby swamp lines the curving, sandy gravel driveway. The frontage is protected by cedar trees that are over thirty-five feet tall that came here as seedlings from the Georgia Forestry Department. Majestic live oaks and water oaks, dot the rolling landscape. Pear trees, overgrown grape vines, fig trees and blueberry bushes are part of the southeast pasture. The courtyard has a Meyer lemon tree and a kumquat tree.

Oxford University

To my delight Daddy retired from New York City and came to Tallahassee to live and help raise his grandson. By now I was a single mother and his presence brought some emotional security as well as practical help to me. I had more freedom to travel at exactly the time I got a chance to go to Oxford University for a study program on Churchill, my hero. Daddy volunteered to do all of the child transporting and supervising and Ophelia was there to see to his daily needs.

Riding the coach from London to Oxford through the hills dotted with manor houses and simple cottages, I felt an exhilaration and a comfort. So many of our ancestors came from there and I felt that connection and continuity, however ephemeral.

Arriving at Tom Tower at Christ Church at dusk, I went directly to Peckwater Quadrangle, Staircase number 9, room 13. The water closet was outside my door. On the same floor, I met Yvonne Starke, attorney for Leon Uris, who wrote *Trinity* and other wonderful books. Chimes rang from Tom Tower. The bells were first used to call the original students inside the safe walled area at night. Overlooking a courtyard from my room, I saw Alice's Garden with a green door going into the Cathedral Garden. Straight out of *Alice's Adventures in Wonderland,* which was written here.

At night I had dinner in the Great Hall and toasted the

Queen's very good health. I went to Evensong each night. I met in the Commons Room with our tutor Copper LeMay, first cousin of General Curtis LeMay. I talked to "Dons," or professors, who were code breakers in World War II along with others who were gamblers, puzzle solvers, and math teachers. I was in heaven.

The bulldogs, campus police, wore bowler hats. We all walked along the river and even went punting on the Thames in big hats and flat bottom boats. The first week I walked down St. Giles Street and got a little plant at the covered market to stick my American flag in. One night we all went to Blue Boar Pub where they cut off the tie of anyone who dared to wear one in, and hang it on the wall. I went to the Randolph Hotel to a tea dance and sipped champagne. I visited Blenheim, ancestral home of Churchill, and saw his sheep and his wonderful art.

I read two deGaulle books about his strange relationship with Churchill. I attended a "Pims" party, so named because the Pims Cocktail is served at such events, in the Masters Garden with dignitaries from around the area. The setting is a miracle of beauty with hollyhocks and stock. Penelope, the tutor's wife, was an architect and explained the spires in the background. The massive square structure known as St. George's Tower was built soon after the 1066 Norman Conquest. Sam Gordon from Napa Valley invited the class out to The Trout for lunch. It was in a 16th Century Inn by the Thames. It was once the guest house of Godstow Nunnery. Swans swam alongside and I could see a waterfall from the patio. I visited Stratford-upon-Avon for

Shakespeare plays and stayed in the rest of the rainy week to do research for class.

The last week at Oxford I was sitting in the Great Hall looking up at the dark paneling with enormous portraits of Cardinal Woolsey and others. It is impossible to convey the size of this hall. Photographs do not do justice. The portrait behind me was larger than a table for eight, yet it seemed normal size. As planned, our class marched into the Great Hall at night as a group, with both brandy glasses and huge cigars as a tribute to Sir Winston, who had both in his hands most of the time. No, we did not light up. There were toasts and speeches.

I went back to the quadrangle to pack up my belongings and gave a lot of things to Margaret, who was my "scout" while there. She brought me tea every morning. I gave her some money and some jewelry. My classmate Sam gave me a silver Churchill bookmark. Yvonne gave me a drawing of the Master's Garden. Slowly I made my way to the coach leaving for London and Gatwick Airport.

The Diamond and the Daffodils

Love had been in the air since I first saw Frank Hughes and we were getting serious about making a life together. In a masterful stroke of family diplomacy, Frank asked my son Lance for permission to marry me. Lance came running upstairs, as I was brushing my hair in my dressing room, and said, breathlessly, "He's going to ask you to marry him! If you don't, you are just crazy." That night after supper Frank gave me a gorgeous diamond engagement ring and I said out loud the "yes" that had always been on my heart.

The next day, and the day after that, our meadow was planted with two thousand daffodil bulbs. As a young boy, Frank had lived and worked on a farm. He knew how to plant and he wasn't afraid to plant anything on a large scale. With knee pads on, and using a dibble to make holes for the bulb, he tamped each bulb individually into the prepared soil along the lane to the house and in some beds in the front yard and near meadow. The fall was the right time to set them out. It was the perfect celebration of our engagement.

Daffodils are a bulb-grown perennial of the narcissus family. The varieties that he planted, Lord Alfred and others, are white, cream and yellow. Some are mixed from the center and petals of the flower. They naturalize, returning year after year. He planted the standard and the pixie varieties, all in full sun. Tallahassee is about as far south as he could have managed them so successfully. Generally they do better in cooler climes, but ours have thrived for decades now.

I have always loved the daffodil as a symbol of spring and because it is such a hopeful little flower. We had seen a beautiful display of them at Callaway Gardens in our early dating days. Frank enjoys nature and he likes doing things for other people. He was also doing something else. He was making an imprint on and a commitment to the place where he would be living the rest of his life. When I came home from work and saw what he was doing, I thought, with tears in my eyes, about how many springs we would enjoy the sight of their arrival together.

The Wedding

I was unbelievably glad to have met my match at 46 years old and had selected an age-appropriate, high-neck Victorian with long sleeve cream lace for the Labor Day wedding to Frank. September 6, 1987, was sunny and clear. We had planned a late morning wedding to accommodate the out-of-towners who had jobs to get back to. We had seen each other for a year. Long enough for Frank to have completely won Daddy over and to be sure that he and my ninth grader son liked each other and would be congenial, that he could live with this teenager and that Lance would share a home with him happily. His son had been to visit and I felt a genuine affection for him.

Since I hadn't met the rest of Frank's family, except for his brother Emmett and wife Sherill, I had decided to cook for them at my own home the night before the wedding when they all arrived in Tallahassee. As an only child, I was quite excited about marrying one of eight. Frank's son Jeff was here from Colorado; sister Laura from Orlando; sister Janie from Palm Springs, California; sister Ann and her husband Forrest and their two daughters Glenna and Stephanie from Marietta, Georgia; and brother Emmett and wife Sherrill from Dothan, Alabama. Even Frank's boss in the Pakistan days, Bill Munson and his wife Vi, came from Texas. My childhood friends who arrived in town, made plans for dinner on their own in a group. It was loud and chaotic at our house on the eve of our wedding. It was comfortable as I put out large pans of lasagna, shrimp creole, huge salads, and hot French bread. We set tables out around the house with wine and checkered tablecloths. Lots of laughter. His family was fun and friendly. *So far so good*, I thought that night.

On the morning of the wedding, my son Lance insisted that he wanted to drive me to the wedding. Since he was a few months short of a driver's license, I stopped about two blocks from the Reidel House, the private home with an exquisite backyard that we had selected for the ceremony. Lance and I switched seats and he drove us to our destination. His best friend, Julian Proctor Crowder, had ridden with us and ceremoniously opened the door for me. Our get-away vehicle was already planned to be Frank's original 1986 CJ-7 Jeep, which we had used on our first date and which Lance and Jennifer later used on their first date and at their wedding. It was a part of the family, later stolen.

Frank and his brother Emmett and son Jeff were waiting. His sisters were upstairs to welcome me and to fluff my hair and check my makeup. Lance's sweetheart Jennifer, who would one day become his wife, was at the wedding. Her parents brought her and she wore a new summer dress made for the event. Tea, lemonade, and cinnamon sticks were served before the wedding. As I came down the stairs with my childhood girlfriends by my side, the pianist Marvin Goldstein and a friend of mine, saxophonist Ned Hafner, played light melodies.

Our sons, brother-in-law Emmett, and my daddy

participated in the ceremony. Each read familiar passages from Corinthians. The only time tears welled up was when my young son, standing straight and tall in his light grey linen jacket said the words, "But when I became a man, I put away childish things."

Afterwards we ate seafood crepes made by my friend Art Smith from Jasper, Florida, who later became private chef for Miss Oprah Winfrey. My dear friend Mary Jane King carved a watermelon with an ocean scene and we had French silk pies and veggie and fruit trays, tiny ham sandwiches and champagne.

That day began a happy family life for all of us and a strong loving influence on Lance's life also. He has an abiding affection for Frank and calls him for most any kind of advice. He particularly relies upon Frank for how to live the life of a good man. As Daddy walked out in the garden with me after the ceremony, he told me that he hadn't wanted to say anything before, but that he was sure I made the right choice.

The Greenbrier

For a birthday gift, Frank sent me to the stately Greenbrier resort, nestled in the Allegheny Mountains of White Sulphur Springs, for a culinary school experience. I was awed by the approach to the palatial facility, the spring house, and the six-foot high floral displays in the public rooms. Falconry classes were offered, for interacting with hawks and falcons and learning the sport of kings. We handled their trained Lanner falcon. The splendor of the lush gardens contrasted with the underground facility that could be reached from inside the kitchen pantry area. A secret government relocation facility was constructed under the mountain under the Greenbrier during the Cold War. It contained a replica of the U. S. Capitol dome which could be photographed during a "press conference" to simulate the president actually speaking from the Capitol. It contained sleeping and survival quarters for the cabinet officers and key members of Congress. It had no provision for spouses or families. It had an auditorium for the Senate and a facility for the House of Representatives to meet. It was eerily impressive.

My own room, designed by Dorothy Draper, was papered in an azalea print with pink and apricot fabric side chairs. I spent very little time in the room. Our chef instructors, Lisa Carter and Riki Senn, worked with us making mozzarella, fashioning little flower shells of phyllo pastry and preparing wine sauces. We were even allowed to pick flowers to use on our tables from the lavish gardens of the Greenbrier. I felt like an imposter when, secateurs in hand, I set out to clip the championship roses for our first meal. Our menu was apple radicchio salad, chicken saltimbocca, couscous pecan mold and bananas foster beignet. Different members of the class prepared each course, served it and explained it.

The guest celebrity chef was Ms. Julia Child, who was set to arrive to talk to our class about two o'clock. I was staying in the kitchen to work on my knife skills while most of the class went to their rooms to freshen up and prepare for the visit of our distinguished guest. She came in early, towering over everyone and laughing and smiling.

Riki said, "Mrs. Swedmark is very tentative in her knife movements."

She, Ms. Julia herself, came directly over to me, grabbed my right arm and held it up. She slammed it down in a chopping motion and said, "Oh! Be courageous!" Even the venerable lady of French cooking advised me to be brave. As soon as she left, I ran up to my room to call my husband and tell him about meeting the grande dame.

Fred Is Murdered

Isn't it amazing how a single phone call can change your life? It could be, "Mrs. Camp you have just won Publisher's Clearinghouse Sweepstakes" or "Gayle, we are pleased to tell you that you passed the bar examination" or "There is a man downstairs with a bouquet of roses." Mine came a few years ago from my husband. I had just left Publix grocery when he called on my car phone. I pushed the button, no hands required model. "Pull over" he said. "I need you to pull over." After arguing that I was fine, I pulled over at the Movie Gallery parking lot and shut off the engine. "Fred is dead, sweetie. They think he may have been murdered. I didn't want you to hear it on the radio."

Fred, my law partner of over thirty years. It had not been a perfect relationship and it never had any romantic overtones, but there was always a respect and affection. Though it was complicated on professional matters, we both felt like members of the same family. He came to see me when I was in labor. He was laughing and wearing a white raincoat. He said, "Man from Glad, Man from Glad," imitating a television commercial to make me smile. We had cried together when he found out his wife had cancer. We had celebrated the weddings of each other's children, taken flights in bad weather to try cases and we had laughed together. I simply could not believe that Fred was dead.

Later that day a helicopter flew over the house. A rumor

circulated that the people we helped to put in jail were threatening all of the partners. The sheriff told me to be extra alert. Mostly I was surprised and shocked and, of course, sad.

Fred had been stabbed at Market Square at lunch. He had staggered into the Tally Grill and said, "Somebody please help me, I have been stabbed." He died before rescue arrived. A man was seen running toward Motel 6.

Over lunch with a sheriff from a nearby county the next day, the opinion expressed at the table was that most likely the killer was long gone on nearby Interstate 10. It was an easy exit from the city and the most likely route of escape.

Three days later a young woman police officer was doing routine patrol on the area on Monroe Street checking tag numbers for a reported stolen vehicle out of Orlando. She saw a man walking across the catwalk at about the same time she called in a stolen truck tag number. She called for backup. The man still had the knife he had plunged into my partner's stomach. He was arrested and convicted. Fred's eldest daughter asked them not to invoke the death penalty. David is serving a life sentence. He had also killed his roommate in Orlando before taking his truck. It was difficult for all of us. Most of all, I think, for his widow and children. I will never forget the phone call.

The College World Series

There are many fine athletes on my mother's side of the family. My precious cousin Annette's son Daniel was one of the best of those. He pitched for Florida State University and broke many records as a closer. His mother and dad and his grandparents stayed with us in Tallahassee a good bit of the time during his college career. His Aunt Cathy, my lovely first cousin from St. Augustine, even came over once or twice. We became closer because of the time spent that way. Uncle Bill, Daniel's grandfather, is mother's much younger baby brother. His wife Catherine, Auntie Cat, is a love who had always been sweet to me. I can remember going out with them when Uncle Bill was courting her. We were happy to become a family again. The College World Series, in Omaha, Nebraska, was still being held in the legendary Rosenblatt Stadium. I was off to Atlanta and Omaha on Delta after a last minute phone call that cousin Daniel had a ticket for me there.

When I called for a room reservation, I found out that all of the hotel rooms in Omaha were gone. Even the bad ones. I was so discouraged. The Chamber of Commerce suggested that I try Iowa. I was a member of the Iowa Bar but I had forgotten my geography. Council Bluffs, Iowa, had a Holiday Inn only three miles to Rosenblatt Stadium across the Missouri River. As I finally walked into the lobby filled with Clemson players in uniform, I yelled, "Go Noles!" I laughed and jumped on the elevator.

As I arrived at the amazing stadium facility, I walked past the Omaha Zoo and passed a bronze statue celebrating sportsmanship and youthful exuberance titled "The Road to Omaha." Flags for each school competing there blew in the breeze above the stadium. Gypsy camps of elaborate tailgating sent some pretty nice aromas my way. The "Raging Cajuns" of Lafayette, Louisiana, had huge pots of gumbo and pitchers of whiskey sours outside the gates. They waved to me and yelled out as I plowed across the rough ditch, "Come and get you some gumbo!"

"Sorry," I said, "I would love to, but I am with FSU."

A bearded guy in khaki shorts yelled, "Shoot, that don't matter. You gonna *need* a drink." The Stanford Cardinal were not as friendly. Yes, they like to be known in the singular. Kevin Costner was sitting with his alma mater Cal State Fullerton, and looked just like one of the dads. Greg Gumble was doing interviews for ESPN. He was more friendly than his brother Bryant and was a little plump but he has a million dollar smile.

As I walked past the television monitors and the fast food vendors to find my relatives, I saw below the exquisitely manicured field and the almost 27,000 fans filling the stadium with the chant: "K time, clap clap." K is the international baseball symbol for strike out and the masses wanted a strike out. FSU was playing Stanford. Before I could sit, a voice over the speaker said, "Martin is signaling for a left-hander." The way he does that is to tap two fingers on the left wrist. That means, "Send me a left-hander from

159

the bull pen." In came Daniel, this young kid who used to throw balls at grandmother's pine trees for hours to learn to hit his spot. He ran into the game as though he couldn't wait to pitch. The batter had three balls and two strikes. Full count. One more strike and Stanford would be out. The crowd noise was fierce. The catcher signaled for a screwball. Not many people throw it anymore, but he knew that Daniel had it in his arsenal. It is a pitch that moves down and away from a right-handed hitter. On a 3-2 count you should throw for a sure strike in case the hitter does not swing at it, but you want to have a lot of movement and be nasty so he can't get a good swing on it.

Daniel warmed up and the batter came back in the box, hit a foul tip to the press box and grinned. It was still a full count. Daniel concentrated. He was ready. He stared at the catcher, wound up, threw this unbelievable screwball and the umpire yelled, "STRIEEEK" We all exhaled.

The announcer said, "This crafty lefty has a future, folks. They tell us this is his first time to pitch in a World Series. Welcome to Omaha, Daniel." Daniel was later drafted by the Philadelphia Phillies.

Art and Music; Music and Art

No doubt about it. There is a need to create. The European poets said it was like a harp in a window with wind gently playing through it. That is how we feel it. Our ancestors painted on the walls of their caves to celebrate a hunt and they decorated their bodies with color to prepare for that hunt. It is not surprising then, that with more leisure, art becomes an outlet for more of us.

Once I was embarrassed when a friend referred to me as a fellow artist. It sounded exaggerated or false somehow. Now I know that we are all artists. It may be knitting or crocheting simple yarn or thread into a beautiful pattern of ridges or valleys. It may be arranging flowers into a wispy garden vision or cooking tidbits with flavor and design. "Children's faces looking up, beholding wonder in a cup," someone wrote. The rainbow is never more gloriously discovered than it is through the eyes of a child. When we are children and are less self-conscious, we just paint and color on freely and draw anything we want and proudly hold up our papers for all the world to see, strangers and friends alike!

Maturity makes us more self conscious. We seek the approval of others. We fear ridicule and so we withdraw. We don't want to be laughed at so we play it safe. We don't experiment so much. As adults we have to remember to find that joy and let out the kid in us.

TWO THOUSAND DAFFODILS

Throughout my busy career I had always found a little time for music but had always felt a need to write music and also to paint and to draw. With a child, civic activities and other things, I never had a chance to explore these fully until my sixties. A new baby grand piano was a dream realized that is a part of my everyday routine now. Then I answered an ad in the paper for a senior art class and met some amazing people who helped me, who shepherded me, some of whom have become close friends. I had found that group of people who knew how to find joy and let the child out to paint. Jan, Lynette, Mary and Jeannette also taught techniques. They convinced me to put my first colored pencil piece in a local show and I got an honorable mention. That was enough to send me on my way.

Soon I had the sun porch full of art supplies, was attending classes out of town, and found a few people who helped me explore watercolors. The result has been fulfilling and satisfying. Bart Frost, Linda Pelc, and Rosemary Ferguson as teachers with totally different styles have shared with me their vision of beauty. Bart, teaching the importance of the underlying sketch and of composition. Linda, in her beginning classes, demonstrating the entire world can be painted with four basic colors: Alizarin crimson, cobalt blue, viridian green and yellow, used in various proportions and mixtures. Rosemary, with her colorful expression of life showing us a certain freedom in creating art. When we were too "uptight" in class she encouraged us to simply drop a paint-filled brush on the paper to show that it would be harmless and maybe even open up new creative avenues for us. All of these people are fine artists and generous teachers. I awaken to walk barefoot on the porch and paint with a cup of coffee in my left hand as the sun comes up. It is a sensation of joy new to me and thoroughly lovely. New friends, new places, new sights have opened to me as I begin to see with the Artist's Eye. Exploring the feminine side of my nature brought new delights and sensations. A part of me that had been thwarted was now evolved and developed. I was fulfilled in a new way that surprised even me.

Alaska

After we were all retired, a bunch of us took that wonderful cruise of the inland passageway to Alaska. Frank and I flew through Salt Lake City to meet friends in Vancouver, British Columbia. We saw Vancouver receding as we pulled away from the dock on the ms Volendam, registered in the Netherlands. The influence of Holland guaranteed premier quality hot chocolate which was handed to us in a mug, together with a warmed woolen blanket, in the early morning if we ventured out to the bow deck to watch calving in Glacier Bay. In various tours we left our beautiful ship and rode tramways, traveled by train, or flew helicopters or floatplanes to explore the glories of Alaska.

Juneau, the state capital, is not accessible by road. It is built on a relatively narrow shelf between towering Mt. Juneau and the deep waters of Gastineau Channel. From there, we rode to the top of Mount Roberts Tramway for a panoramic view emblematic of the area. We flew by floatplane to the remote and historic Taku Glacier Lodge for a spectacular lunch of salmon cooked outside over alder wood. Our hostess in the cozy but primitive log cabin made sourdough bread and gave us fresh tea poured over glacier ice a thousand years old or more.

In Skagway we climbed aboard a train, the legendary White Pass Summit Scenic Railway, to visit the peaks that challenged the miners of the Klondike Gold Rush of the

1890s. Back in Skagway, we saw the gravesite of "Soapy Smith," con artist who had swindled new arrivals and was killed in a shoot-out in 1898. The town, touristy at best, had many saloons. Some were authentic and some were not.

In Ketchikan we made a serious attempt to study the totem poles. They are on street corners, in parks, and at the visitors center. We went to the historic Ketchikan section where the totem poles are found at Totem Heritage Center, Totem Bight State Park. We rode out to the village of Saxman to learn a little about Tlingit culture. We entered a Tlingit clan house with reverence. A picturesque cannery row lines the city limits, a result of the abundant salmon there. In the heart of town a rambling boardwalk built on pilings comprises the infamous red-light district at Ketchikan Creek. Dolly Arthur, lady of the night, has her famous house preserved as a museum.

There were many experiences to remember forever. Some can be seen in travel guides and films. Some cannot. The last night of the cruise when our men were dressed for dinner like Cary Grant, Frank put a small blue gift box at the foot of our bed. As we started to walk out to dinner he said, "I wanted you to have a memento of our cruise." He handed me the tanzanite necklace he had purchased for me in Ketchikan. He was right. Every time I wear it I think of dancing with him after dinner under the clear open sky and stars of Alaska.

A Walk Through the Valley
of the Shadow of Death

At a time when I felt pretty good, had new interests and a great marriage, I was shocked to hear that I had to come back to radiology for the fourth time. I had scheduled a trip to my hometown to attend the 150th anniversary of my little hometown church. I went ahead as planned.

Somehow, the trip was strangely appropriate to prepare me for what was coming. I sat in the little wooden church with Bill, Andy and Tommy and their wives Sally, Trina, and Lyn and watched as my former Sunday school teacher came in and screamed with delight at seeing us all there together again.

We had beautiful music to sing and ceremonies to perform and a Communion Service together. We sang old songs like "I'll Fly Away" and "To God Be The Glory," which we Presbyterians used to call the Methodists' national anthem. We listened to familiar voices. Daddy used to love to sing the Doxology loud and off key. Memories of him came pouring in as I looked at the wonderful old pipe organ and simple cross hanging in the center of the sanctuary. The cross, I remembered, had been given in memory of a young minister named Croms who had drowned in the surf at the beach while successfully saving a young Valdosta tourist. That bell has a history also. It was taken down, during the

Civil War to be melted into material for weapons. A Yankee major saved it. "You put that back up!" he said. "We are not yet that desperate." He married the minister's daughter after the war.

Our church building is an architectural style called New England Meeting House. Simple. Lovely. During the Second World War it was accidentally hit with live ammunition when an exercise from the Jacksonville Naval Air Squadron practiced over Fernandina and went badly wrong. My childhood friend Tommy, now a retired TWA pilot, lived next door. He had gotten up early to walk to his grandpa's for breakfast and was spared when the shells went through the roof of his house and his pillow. You can still see the areas in the brick streets of town where the shells hit. We were all spared. Our beloved church was spared. Now I was going home to Tallahassee, hoping to be spared again.

To spend that time at the church of my childhood, my baptism, was a fitting prelude to the next week. I drove home full of faith in the future for whatever might be. I am not crazy enough to want to die, but I am not afraid of death. I simply would enjoy postponing it a bit. Driving home I was peaceful, but I did suspect something was up. Coming back for my May 30 appointment, I had sense enough to know that it was not good when they suggested that I might want to bring my husband.

"The news is not good," Dr. Carr said.

I felt like a cat had run over my grave and that all the air was sucked out of the room. Frank and I handled it calmly and maturely. We immediately started talking about what I had to do. We made plans. Surgery was first and proved more complicated than expected. My son's mother-in-law Sue helped to usher me through this phase and was in surgery with me. Knowing that was immensely comforting. My daughter-in-law was holding my hand in the recovery room when I awoke. Both of these women are dedicated nurse practitioners, but more than that, they are caring and kind. They were there for me in every way possible.

After the pain of surgery and post surgery I began that rugged regime of chemotherapy. I try to make this tolerable but do not blame those who want to skip the section on illness. I wasn't crazy about it but tried to make it work. Always positive, I packed a little "beach bag" to take to my chemotherapy sessions since they lasted for hours. I took note paper, magazines, and even hard candies to fight off the nausea. I rearranged the doctor's reception room to make it more attractive. I took cookies to the staff. Anything to keep spirits up and to make it bearable for all of us. For one year our life was sad and a little bit of hell in spite of our good intentions.

Cancer is a family disease. My husband was as kind as anyone could be. I hated the sad look in his eyes when he didn't know I was looking. I hated for him to have to take over chores. He never once made me feel that he resented it, but I didn't like to be helpless after some of the chemotherapy laid me out flat. I lost my hair and I didn't cry. I saw it go down the drain and was surprised that I did not hate that part. Maybe I wasn't vain enough. I was concentrating on simply surviving. My husband told me one of the kindest things I have ever heard a person say to another. He said, "You know, you have a perfectly shaped head. I never would have noticed it with all the hair on it." He made it sound like a good thing that I was bald. He told me I was pretty. My friend Ann and my friend Carolyn combed the stores to find attractive scarves and head covers for me. Fran discovered the softest fabric to keep my shoulders from being chilled. Ann Camp made her mother's egg custard and came out with her little dog, Minnie, just to "check on me." Mason brought peanut butter cookies. Nella brought soup. My art class friends came and we ate lunch here. They brought ice cream sundae makings and they set the table. I got wigs to wear to the grocery store once I was able. After chemotherapy I went to radiation every single weekday at the hospital for over two months. I saw people who were hopeless and tried to keep them company. I always thought I had a chance. I never thought "Why me?" I only thought, "Why not me?" The low spots came when friends and fellow patients died and when my arm swelled up from lymphedema and I had to wear rubber shields all the way up to my shoulder. When I tried to play the piano and couldn't because my fingers were so swollen, I cried. I tried to play when the house was empty because it sounded like a child beating her fist on the keys sometimes.

The high spots were when Frances and Carolyn came from Fernandina, my hometown, just to take me to lunch. When the class of '57 sent a great looking eyelet robe to me. When I had precious notes from my cheerleader squad or men and women who had sat by me in algebra or civics.

These lifted me up. Prayers of my Christian friends lifted me up. My faith was there for me.

Eventually the fog lifted. Hair and energy came back. Some of the tests even looked better. I was able to counsel with other people in this special sorority of challenges. Was there a purpose for all of this? I honestly do not know. If I am able to help others, I wish I could say that it was worth the suffering. It wasn't. Still, it is a side benefit that I am willing to share.

My Seventieth Birthday

Frank, ever the celebrator of birthdays, surprised me with a reservation at Amelia Island Plantation, the fanciest of resorts in my hometown, to honor my seventieth. I bought new sandals. I splurged on an appointment with the popular Patricia Grimes for a great haircut and highlights. I carried the copy of the reservation around with me in my purse for weeks. It was even more magical than I fantasized. The suite at the Inn was absolutely beautiful, with nice art on the walls and beautiful fabrics on the chairs and bed coverings. Although I can scarcely believe that 70 years old is the right number, I was happy to be in my favorite town for that event. The weather was perfectly glorious. My dearest friends took me to a lovely Victorian house in downtown Fernandina to a restaurant called 29 South for lunch of lobster. Frank took me to The Veranda at the Plantation for dinner of sea bass with some close friends. Both were exquisite. There was also time for quiet meditation. I wrote this on that day:

First Footprints

It is the morning of my seventieth birthday and I am barefoot and alone on the white sands of my childhood, now tinted peach from the sun beginning to rise up and meet the day. Pink shadows make free form designs on the dunes.

There are no footprints on this southeast end of the barrier island called Amelia. Here, directly across the inlet from Big Talbot Island, there are no cabanas, no beach bars, only the sweet gentle rhythm of an outgoing tide firming up the strand beneath me. The lulling sound calms me. Two lazy dolphins playing offshore show their dorsal fins.

I am celebrating in this sacred place where eagles nest, where migratory birds land and feed from a bountiful table. Where sponges and sand dollars decorate the sands next to ancient uprooted trees. Where I played Robinson Crusoe as a little girl.

A wooded path goes inland and I follow it to tall cabbage palms, to magnolias and to live oaks. It is cool in here. In the distance red foxes make their morning call and bobcats climb to search for breakfast.

Leaving these coastal woods, I see the slow graceful glide of the osprey above. I inhale the salt air, and feel cleansed. I breathe the precious memories of this place and become that barefoot child again.

Epilogue

I am guessing that everyone has a story. I imagine that everyone has a cross to bear. Everyone has some happiness and joy. Sharing these with others seems to help. Shared joys. Shared sorrows.

I am not perfect but I am more sane than I have any right to be. Support and love came from some of my family, the friends who have loved me, Anna and Ophelia who came into my households at the right time, "Aunt Ruth" who nurtured me, and my abiding faith. The paperweight from Anna is still with me and sits on the side table by my bed. It reminds me to fear nothing.

Each of us is born with only the fear of falling. All other fears are learned. We have to find armor to fend those fears off and to live freely. We have to find weapons to survive.

We are born into a kind of insulated solitary confinement and we spend most of our lives sending out an S.O.S, hoping to God that somebody will hear us.

If they know us and love us just as we are, we are Blessed. I am Blessed.

Acknowledgments

My editor and publisher, Wild Women Writers' Donna Meredith, has made this effort possible. Without her patience, expert advice and professionalism this book would not be in print today.

The resource material gathered by my cousin John Bentley Mayes for his excellent book, "Power in the Blood," was useful to me in every way.

The friends who read the material and made suggestions—son Lance and daughter-in-law Jennifer, Ann Camp, Bruce and Jeannette Buckley, Carolyn Oxley Grafton—can never be thanked sufficiently. I am so happy they helped.

My writers' group, Writing for Fun, shepherded by the poet Betsy Alexander, has been encouraging my writing for some years. Thank you all so much.

My law partners Carl Peterson and John Jolly and associates Keith Tischler and Barbara Fromm made the practice of law the joy that it is meant to be. It has been a wonderful ride! Thank you all.